TECH IN THE TRENCHES

Strategic Inventions of the Korean War

Cathleen Small

Cavendish Square

New York

Published in 2017 by Cavendish Square Publishing, LLC
243 5th Avenue, Suite 136, New York, NY 10016

First Edition

Website: cavendishsq.com

CPSIA Compliance Information: Batch #CW17CSQ

Library of Congress Cataloging-in-Publication Data

Names: Small, Cathleen, author.
Title: Strategic inventions of the Korean War / Cathleen Small.
Description: New York : Cavendish Square Publishing, [2017] |
Series: Tech in the trenches | Includes bibliographical references and index.
Identifiers: LCCN 2016022257 | ISBN 9781502623454 (library bound) |
ISBN 9781502623461 (E-book)
Subjects: LCSH: Korean War, 1950-1953--Equipment and supplies--United States. |
United States. Army--Equipment--History--20th century--Juvenile literature. |
Military weapons--United States--History--20th century--Juvenile literature.
Classification: LCC DS919 .S54 2017 | DDC 951.904/21--dc23
LC record available at https://lccn.loc.gov/2016022257

Editorial Director: David McNamara
Editor: Kristen Susienka
Copy Editor: Nathan Heidelberger
Associate Art Director: Amy Greenan
Designer: Jessica Nevins
Production Assistant: Karol Szymczuk
Photo Researcher: J8 Media

The photographs in this book are used by permission and through the courtesy of: Cover The US Army/Helicopter Hoist/Flickr.com; pp. 4, 22, 25,48, 55, 58, 79, 92 Bettman/Getty Images; p. 7 Time Life Pictures/US Army/The LIFE Picture Collection/Getty Images; p. 9 Lisa Larsen/The LIFE Picture Collection/Getty Images; p. 10 Keystone/Hulton Archive/Getty Images; p. 13 The LIFE Picture Collection/Getty Images; p. 18 Carl Mydans/The LIFE Picture Collection/Getty Images; p. 26 Hulton Archive/Archive Photos; p. 29 Hulton Archive/Getty Images; p. 34 Wikimedia Commons/File:Flak jacket 1942.jpg; p. 37 Planet News Archive/SSPL/Getty Images; p. 40 SuperStock/Getty Images; p. 51 marcociannarel/Shutterstock.com; p. 57 Stocktrek Images/Getty Images; p. 62 national Archies and Records Administration/Wikimedia Commons/File:Charles R Drew portrait.jpg; p. 68 Interim Archives/Archive Photos/Getty Images; p. 71 Wikimedia Commons/File:T¬34¬85¬korea.jpg; p. 74 Terry Fincher/Hulton Archive/Getty Images; p. 77 Ira Gay Sealy/Denver Post/Getty Images; p. 84 Echo/Cultura/Getty Images; p. 87 Robert Nickelsberg/Archive Photos/Getty Images; p. 90 Christopher Furlong/Getty Images; p. 96 Paula Bronstein/Getty Images; p. 99 Nesterenko Maxym/Shutterstock.com.

Printed in the United States of America

CONTENTS

August 1950: US Marine troops arriving in Pusan, Korea.

INTRODUCTION

Changing Times Lead to War

The Korean War broke out in June 1950. It was a rather strange time in United States history. The country had gotten out of World War II five years before, so Americans were in the process of rebuilding their lives. World War II had been long and devastating, and people were still trying to make sense of the atrocities that had occurred in Europe and the Pacific.

Meanwhile, the Cold War was emerging. The Cold War itself didn't involve hand-to-hand combat, like World War II had, but it was a frightening time. It was a time of political maneuvering and never-ending threats of nuclear war. Who had nuclear weapons, and where? Who would be the first to deploy them? Could the United States stop its enemies from deploying them?

It was also a time of blossoming knowledge about Communism. The Soviet Union had been the United States' ally in fighting against Hitler, but they were a Communist nation, and that scared a lot of people—civilians and politicians alike. The United States' capitalist society was in stark contrast to the Communist society of the Soviet Union, and the United States feared that eventually Communist nations such as the Soviet Union would swallow up non-Communist nations and grow their power.

Early 1950—right before the Korean War broke out—was also a time of trust in the government. Although many Americans had died, the bottom line was that the United States had led its soldiers through World War II and had won. Hitler was no longer in power, Nazis were no longer a massive threat, and the conflict posed by Japan had been dealt with as well. Most Americans trusted the government to make appropriate decisions about involvement in war and how to run the military.

That would change not long after the Korean War, of course. The Vietnam War came just after the end of the Korean War, and it was an incredibly unpopular conflict. Americans lost their faith in the government and felt as though the country was fighting a war in which they didn't belong.

So the Korean War was sandwiched right between that generation of Americans who believed in their government and believed in fighting for the cause, and the generation of Americans who felt they had no place in a war that didn't directly affect American soil. Thus, the Korean War was somewhat forgotten.

People celebrate the end of World War II in Paris in 1945.

Many people supported it, but then some people didn't. In general, people didn't feel particularly strongly about it one way or the other. It wasn't a part of their daily consciousness because it wasn't widely televised, and because the American public hadn't yet grown fully distrustful of the government, the Korean War didn't turn into the impassioned issue that the Vietnam War did. Moreover, because there was no one evil face of the Korean War, like Hitler had been during World War II, there wasn't necessarily the visceral reaction to the atrocities of the war that had occurred with World War II.

Whether it was visible or not, the Korean War occurred, and it took many lives, as wars do. It took military lives and it took civilian lives. When it ended after just three years, a lot of people had died. The lack of visibility didn't mean there was a lack of death.

But the death toll was actually lessened during the Korean War, in part due to the technological innovations that took place surrounding the war. Major advances were made in treating injuries and in wartime medical care, and they saved thousands of lives. Protective gear took a step forward in usefulness and in protection level, which also saved the lives of countless soldiers. Moreover, as typically happens during a war, weaponry took a step forward as well.

In the end, the Korean War was a time of loss but also a time of gain. The inventions made during the conflict went on to benefit future generations in future times of combat; some of them even changed the face of war as we know it.

While the Korean War may have been somewhat faceless, lurking quietly in the background, it was not without its contributions to the military and to society. Certainly, men serving in the Vietnam War, which came soon thereafter, benefited from the advances made during the Korean War. Indeed, some of the innovations of the Korean War have informed military practices of today as well.

When the Korean War broke out, most Americans still had faith in the government's decisions about war and the military. That faith would later be tested by the Vietnam War.

The Korean War may be the Forgotten War for Americans, but it certainly was remembered by those directly affected in Korea.

CHAPTER ONE

The Forgotten War

Officially, the Korean War began on June 25, 1950. That was the day that North Korean tanks crossed the border into South Korea, carrying roughly seventy-five thousand soldiers. A few days later, the United States joined South Korea in the fight against North Korea.

AMERICA IN THE EARLY 1950s

In the late 1940s and very early 1950s, America was in a period of peaceful recovery from the horrors of World War II. Many soldiers had been killed, of course, and families left behind were beginning to rebuild their lives. More importantly, soldiers who were fortunate enough to return home began to rebuild their lives on American soil. The wives who had stayed home while their husbands went off to war settled back into the domesticity of the **American Dream**, and the women who had actively worked for the war effort either chose to continue working in some capacity or set about reentering domestic life. The reunification of families even led to a massive baby boom. It was a time of rebuilding and of hope.

Over all of that growth and prosperity and hope, however, hung clouds of concern. There is never a time of total peace, and such was the case in this era. The beginnings of the Cold War were emerging, and the tensions between North and South Korea were an ever-present reminder of the threat of war.

THE KOREAN WAR IN A NUTSHELL

Korea had been a divided nation for some time. When World War II ended in 1945, Korea was divided into two halves. Prior to that, since 1910, Korea had been part of the Japanese empire. When Japan fell in World War II, the United States and the Soviets decided to divide the country along the 38th parallel, with the Soviets occupying

The 38th parallel is the dividing line between Communist North Korea and non-Communist South Korea.

Communist North Korea and the United States occupying South Korea. In 1948, the two halves each had a designated government: South Korea was ruled by the Republic of Korea, under the leadership of Syngman Rhee, and North Korea was ruled by the

People's Democratic Republic of Korea, under the leadership of Kim Il Sung.

As is often the case in such divisions of a country, relations between the two governments were strained. It took only two years for tensions to become strong enough for North Korea to advance beyond the 38th parallel, which marked the border between the two regions, and invade South Korea.

After President Harry Truman authorized American troops to enter the fight on behalf of South Korea, the United Nations authorized fifteen of its member nations to join the United States in the fight. At first, progress was very slow. The Korean People's Army of North Korea gained considerable ground and forced the South Koreans far into the Pusan Perimeter, at the southeastern tip of the Korean Peninsula. The South Korean army was no match for the well-trained North Korean army, and many US troops fell ill from drinking contaminated water from **rice paddies** in the hot, dry Korean summer. In addition, the first US forces that were sent to South Korea were part of the Twenty-Fourth Infantry Division of the Eighth United States Army, which had been stationed in Japan and which had rather outdated equipment, thanks to cutbacks in defense spending by the Truman administration.

However, slowly but surely, as more troops arrived under United States general Douglas MacArthur, the South Korean troops were able to make headway and begin pushing back against the North Korean troops that had pushed far into South Korea. By this point, the North Koreans were suffering from

Early Battles and the Need for Advancements in Medical Care

Losses of life, serious injuries, and poor health plagued the forces during the Korean War. Health problems were particularly an issue for the US troops fighting in South Korea, as their gastrointestinal tracts were unprepared for the contaminants in the water they drank from the rice paddies of the region. In some cases, the paddies were fertilized with human waste, and when the soldiers drank the contaminated water, they fell ill.

The early engagements of the Korean War, although small, proved particularly deadly. For example, the Battle of Osan, which was a very early American engagement in the war, left 180 people dead, wounded, or taken prisoner, out of only 540 soldiers dispatched to the battle.

In World War II, nurses and doctors had played important roles in the military, tending to as many wounded as they could. But clearly, advancements in military health care were much needed. The Korean War ultimately marked a time of development in health care for the military, with the introduction of medevac helicopters used to transport the ill or wounded, and with mobile army surgical hospitals (MASH) being established for on-ground treatment of the sick and wounded. In addition, in 1951 the Armed Forces Blood Donor Program was established to meet the need for more blood to transfuse into those wounded in the war.

massive losses of troops, plus a shortage of supplies. The South Koreans then made steady progress until late November 1950, when Communists from China, under the leadership of Mao Zedong, joined the North Koreans in their fight. The Chinese were responding to what they felt was American intrusion when President Truman sent troops to the Taiwan Strait to prevent an invasion by the People's Republic of China. Together, Chinese forces and the Korean People's Army (KPA) pushed back into South Korea, winning such battles as the Chinese New Year's Offensive, in which the KPA attacked at night and disoriented South Korean forces and United Nations (UN) forces by using loud trumpets and gongs. By January, the KPA had recaptured Seoul, the capital of South Korea.

South Korea fought back, though, and under the direction of General MacArthur they were able to push the North Korean forces back to the 38th parallel. From mid-1951 to the end of the war in mid-1953, the fighting remained around the 38th parallel, with neither army gaining significant ground in the other's territory. There were numerous battles fought, but the two sides were essentially deadlocked in a stalemate.

Although initially successful as a leader for the South Korean forces, General MacArthur was outspoken in his criticism of US policy. President Truman believed that mounting an aggressive approach toward North Korea would escalate the war, which could spell death for millions of innocent people, thanks to the threat of deployment of nuclear weapons. General MacArthur, on the other hand, felt that attempts to secure peace with North Korea were, in effect, giving in to Communist wishes, which he found unacceptable. MacArthur sent a letter detailing his pro-war stance to House Republican leader Joseph Martin, who leaked the letter to the press. This led President Truman to remove General MacArthur from command on April 11, 1951, when he fired him for insubordination. General Matthew B. Ridgway was appointed commander in chief, and General James Van Fleet took over command of the army.

Skirmishes along the 38th parallel continued until July 27, 1953, when North and South Korea signed an **armistice** that formed a new boundary between the two regions, established the 2-mile-wide (3.2-kilometer-wide) Korean Demilitarized Zone, and allowed prisoners of war to be returned. Despite the armistice, though, in the more than five decades since, no peace treaty has been signed. Technically, the two halves of Korea are still in conflict.

The Korean War didn't get as much US attention as World War II did and as the Vietnam War did later—in fact, the Korean War is sometimes called the Forgotten War or the Unknown War. However, despite its relative anonymity, the Korean War was still unpopular among Americans. Although exact numbers do not exist, it is estimated that nearly 40,000 US troops died, and 103,000 more were wounded. Korean and Chinese casualties were exponentially higher, resulting in a death toll of soldiers and civilians numbering in the millions—quite high for a war that

A Force to Be Reckoned With

General Douglas MacArthur had a storied military career. He came by his military background naturally—his father was a senior ranking officer in the army, and MacArthur graduated from the United States

General Douglas MacArthur remains a vital character in the history of the Korean War.

Military Academy at West Point with highest honors. Later, he was superintendent at West Point.

He held several high positions during World War I. MacArthur actually retired from the army in 1937 but was recalled to active duty during World War II, where he was in charge of the Southwest Pacific Theatre. He served in post–World War II Japan, and he was in charge of UN troops at the beginning of the Korean War.

One of MacArthur's great achievements during his time in command of UN forces in Korea was the Battle of Inchon, which took place from September 15 to September 19, 1950. It was an **amphibious** attack that was an early victory for the UN forces, and it ultimately led South Korea to recapture Seoul. The battle was quite large, involving seventy-five thousand troops, and it was a decisive victory for the UN forces.

However, MacArthur's victories were not enough to save him from ultimate dismissal from his position. President Truman officially terminated MacArthur from his post on April 11, 1951, citing insubordination. Although personal opinions on the matter vary, few would disagree that MacArthur was a strong personality. As historian David McCullough noted, "There was nothing bland about him, nothing passive about him, nothing dull about him." He was known to be extremely intelligent and dedicated to serving his country, but he was also seen by some as egotistical, aloof, and imperious. His views on the war differed significantly from Truman's, and MacArthur wasn't afraid to voice his opinions. Ultimately, his outspokenness led to his dismissal.

lasted about three years. In fact, the civilian casualties from the Korean War were higher than civilian casualties in World War II or the Vietnam War.

The unpopularity of the war proved profitable for one person: Dwight D. Eisenhower, who pledged during his presidential campaign to end the war. Indeed, under the administration of Eisenhower, the armistice was signed and a tentative peace was enacted, even if the two countries were still technically at odds.

THE COLD WAR

The United States might not have been so quick to join in the war if it weren't for the link the skirmishes had to the greater Cold War. The Cold War began after the end of World War II. Technically, the United States and the Soviet Union had been allies in the fight against Nazi Germany. However, after World War II, the relationship between the two allies became tense. The United States feared the spread of Communism from the Soviet Union, which established pro-Communist government holds in several countries in Eastern Europe. As a democracy, the United States felt that there was potential danger in the spread of Communism.

Things grew more tense in 1947 when the Truman Doctrine was established to offer aid to governments fighting against Communism and when the Marshall Plan provided economic assistance to Western European countries with potentially unstable political structures that might fall prey to Communist takeover. Thus began a tense, quiet standoff, with the Soviets holding control over a number of Eastern European nations and the United States supporting the non-Communist efforts of Western European nations.

The Soviets scored a major prize when Communist forces won the Chinese Civil War. China, with its massive population, became an ally for the Soviets. Together, they formed a huge Communist front in the East.

The initial North Korean invasion on June 25, 1950, was considered the first military action of the Cold War. The United States and its allies felt that if they didn't take action, it might lead to bigger problems down the road. If the Soviets took over Korea, what next? Would they continue to move on, swallowing up countries until suddenly there was a much larger Communist stake in the world than the United States was comfortable with? As President Truman stated, "If we let Korea down, the Soviet[s] will keep right on going and swallow up one [place] after another." In his autobiography, Truman remembered, "I felt certain that if South Korea was allowed to fall, Communist leaders would be emboldened to override nations closer to our own shores. If the Communists were permitted to force their way into the Republic of Korea without opposition from the free world, no small nation would have the courage to resist threats and aggression by stronger Communist neighbors."

Remember, this was not even a decade after the end of World War II. Americans and their allies had just watched as Hitler and the Nazi forces systematically took over massive parts of Europe, starting slowly and gaining more and more ground,

Air-raid drills during the Korean War sent schoolchildren and teachers taking cover under desks and tables whenever the sirens were heard.

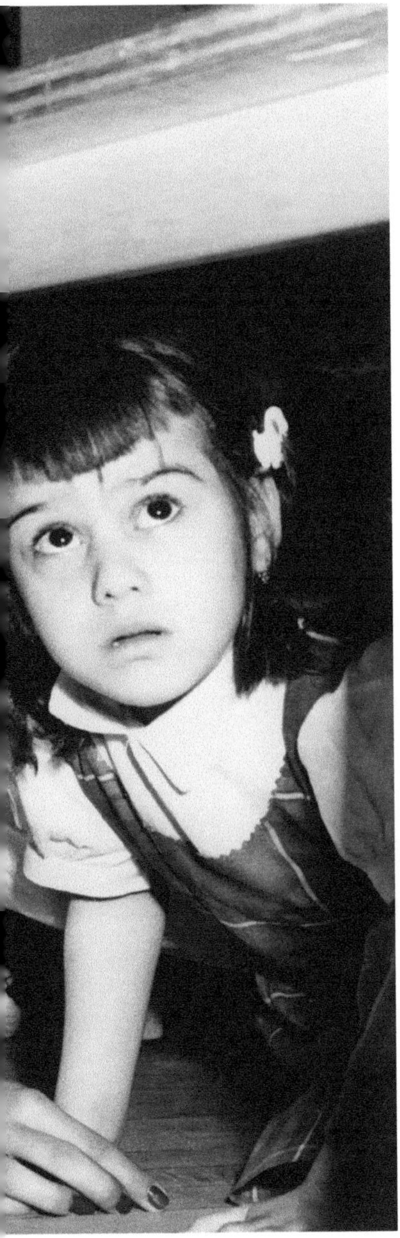

as millions of lives were lost and global security was threatened. If the United States allowed South Korea to fall to the Communists, could a similar situation happen again?

Likewise, nuclear weapons were becoming part of the story. The atomic bombs dropped on Hiroshima and Nagasaki had opened people's eyes to the possibility of mass destruction in one fell swoop. If the Communists gained too much ground, what risk did that present for the non-Communist nations? The United States was concerned that if they didn't make some sort of peace with the North Koreans, it could spell war with the Soviets or Communist China—or even World War III. With World War II so fresh in people's memories, it was not a possibility the US government was willing to entertain.

The Cold War ended up lasting long past the official end of the Korean War, and the US fear of a "domino effect," whereby the fall of one nation to Communism might lead to the fall of more nations to Communism, was a constant concern. Indeed, it was a factor in the much longer and larger Vietnam War, which followed not long after the end of the Korean War. It also figured into US tensions with Cuba, leading to the Cuban Missile Crisis in the early 1960s. It was a major talking point in presidential elections in the 1950s and 1960s, as Americans feared Communist takeover and nuclear war.

In short, the Cold War was on everyone's mind, and ignoring the tensions in Korea was not an option in the minds of the United States government. A stand needed to be taken if the United States was to maintain its place in the Cold War.

WAR AND INVENTION

War brings about death and destruction, for sure, but it also tends to bring about pockets of prosperity and innovation. Jobs open up in times of war, and the existence of war breeds the necessity for invention. So while the history of war can be gloomy and depressing, it can also be fascinating to look at from a standpoint of innovation. Like many other wars, the Korean War brought the loss of life, but it also brought the gain of invention.

People on Wall Street in New York City take cover during an air-raid drill, circa 1951.

Helicopters bring troops to the battlefield during the Korean War.

CHAPTER TWO

The Need for Change

Life in general is an ongoing process of learning from mistakes and making improvements. If we never made mistakes, we would never develop and refine the finer points of our lives. The same is true in war and conflict: We learn from what went well and, perhaps more importantly, what *didn't* go well. And then the next time conflict comes around—or, ideally, before it happens—we learn from what didn't go well, and we refine our process for greater success the next time around.

So it was with the Korean War. To understand the need for improvements in processes and technology, it helps to look at the climate of the world shortly before the war began. In particular, it helps to look at World War II, which had ended just five years before, and to look at the emerging Cold War.

THE POST–WORLD WAR II CLIMATE

World War II was a victory for the Allies, which included both the United States and the Soviet Union, though the two would soon experience tension. In the end, the United States and its allies emerged victorious. Hitler had been removed from power, the countries he had taken over had been liberated, and the conflict with Japan had ended with the atomic bombs dropped on Hiroshima and Nagasaki and the subsequent surrender of Japan.

However, the victory was a bloody, costly one. Estimates on the total number of Americans killed in World War II vary, but according to the National World War II Museum, 418,500 Americans died in World War II, with 416,800 of those deaths being military personnel. Nearly half a million casualties from one war, which the United States had officially been involved in for less than four years. Worldwide, it is believed that around sixty million people died during World War II. Although there are no certain numbers, it is believed that around forty million people were injured or killed in battle. The death toll from the atomic bombs was also staggering, but it is believed that if the Allies had invaded Japan by more conventional means, the death toll would've been much greater.

Clearly, improved medical care was a must. There was no way everyone injured in battle could be saved, of course, but there had to be ways to reduce the incredible death toll. This was one of the main areas where impressive gains in technology and process were made between the end of World War II and the onset of the

A medic attends to a wounded soldier in Normandy, France, in 1944. New advances in care and treatment of the wounded during the Korean War would lead to fewer losses in lives.

Korean War—numerous developments in treatment and medical care took place.

But better medical care was a defense, more or less—it addressed caring for soldiers after they were hurt. What about before they were wounded? Was there a way to protect soldiers so that the numbers of those critically wounded might not be so high? Protecting soldiers on the battlefield and in the skies was another priority for the military.

But again, that's defense: How best to protect soldiers as they fight for our country? There is a saying that the best defense is a strong offense. In fact, it is one of the nine principles of war followed by the United States military, and it's known as the strategic offensive principle. The idea is that a strong offense will unsettle the enemy—and if the enemy is busy protecting itself from a strong offense, it won't have the time or resources to launch its own attack. So offense was key, too. The United States needed to focus on improving their offense as well as their defense. Indeed, they did make significant gains in this area by introducing a much-improved weapon that had been used with some success in World War II but was used with much greater success during the Korean War.

THE EMERGING COLD WAR

As World War II came to a close in 1945, the first steps into a new conflict were being taken. The United States and much of the rest of the world were about to enter a rather nebulous conflict known as the Cold War.

The dates for the Cold War are somewhat vague, since it wasn't an official declared war or conflict—rather, it was a state of political unrest and tension between two groups known as the Western Bloc and the Eastern Bloc. The Western Bloc was made up of the United States and its **NATO** allies, which were mostly in northern and western Europe. The Eastern Bloc consisted of the Communist Soviet Union and its allies in the **Warsaw Pact**, which included several countries in central and eastern Europe. The Western and Eastern Blocs were symbolically separated by the **Iron Curtain**, which formed an imaginary dividing line between the regions. Although no exact dates can be agreed upon, it's generally established that the Cold War took place from roughly 1947 to roughly 1991, with the first major conflict of the Cold War being the Korean War.

The politics behind the Cold War are incredibly complex and warrant a book of their own (indeed, many such books have been published!), but in the most basic of terms, the Cold War occurred when the uneasy alliance between the United States and the Soviet Union, which had been formed in their fight against the Nazis in World War II, broke down. The United States was—and is—a capitalistic, democratic society, and the Soviet Union was a Communist nation informed by the principles of **Marxism** and **Leninism**, which were socialist in nature and dictated a single political party and state control over the economy.

After World War II, the United States and the Soviet Union split up various territories, and those that the Soviet Union controlled were under Communist rule. Perhaps most famously, this included Germany, which was split into East and West Germany. The city of Berlin, Germany, was actually physically split by the massive Berlin Wall, with West Berlin being part of the Western Allies (and generally aligned with the politics of West Germany) and East Berlin being part of East Germany and the Communist Bloc. East Germany was under the control of the Communist Soviet Union, and West Germany was a federal republic under NATO, and thus an ally of the United States.

A similar split occurred in Korea, among other places. Korea, which had been ruled by Japan until the end of World War II, was split in two. North Korea became a Communist nation supported by the Soviet Union and China (also newly a Communist nation), and South Korea became the Republic of Korea and was supported by the United States and ultimately the United Nations.

The Cold War itself didn't involve any combat between the major powers—it was simply political disagreement and military unrest. But associated with the Cold War were numerous physical conflicts, and the Korean War was one of them—the first major one, in fact. What made the Cold War loom so large in the minds of many was the fact that nuclear weapons were involved. Both the Soviets and the United States had access to nuclear weapons, so the threat of all-out nuclear war loomed large. The nuclear weapons were both a threat and a safety—neither side *wanted* an all-out nuclear war, so neither wanted to fire the first shot, so to speak. Both sides were invested in this careful dance of power that ensured that no one had to resort to deployment of nuclear weapons.

The public knew the dangers of nuclear war. They had seen the effects of the atomic bombs dropped on Hiroshima and Nagasaki, which collectively killed well over one hundred thousand people. The initial blast in Hiroshima immediately destroyed nearly 70 percent of the city and killed around eighty thousand people. Many people died after the fact due to nuclear fallout. The Cold War involved several decades of political maneuvering to ensure an uneasy stalemate in which neither side detonated the nuclear weapons at their fingertips. The potential cost was simply too great.

TECHNOLOGICAL DEVELOPMENTS

To minimize casualties and maximize their offensive during the Korean War, the United States explored a number of new ideas, which resulted in major technological developments.

Flak Vests

On the defensive side, the United States continued to work to develop more wearable bulletproof body armor, which became known as flak vests and flak jackets. Body armor had existed for many centuries, but it tended to be too heavy for soldiers to wear comfortably, and it wasn't entirely effective, particularly in the face of modern warfare. It generally protected against knife and sword wounds, for example, but modern wars weren't really fought with knives and swords. Artillery was the name of the game, and body armor as it had existed for centuries couldn't stop a bullet or the

A Russian soldier wears a flak vest during World War II. This armor was no match for the ammunition used during the Korean War, thus calling for advances in armor technology during that conflict.

shrapnel or debris from a grenade or land mine. So, the United States invested time and money into developing a more effective, more wearable form of body armor. They ended up with two main types of flak vests that were much more suitable for combat wear than previous versions had been.

Medical Developments

As mentioned, the casualties in World War II were staggering. With the Cold War involving the ever-present threat of a nuclear strike, the military had to be prepared for large-scale injury and death. So, improving medical care, conditions, and treatment for the injured was a must.

The American Red Cross

The American Red Cross was instrumental in helping to organize the blood-banking program set up during the Korean War, but the organization had a long history before that. It was founded in 1881 by nurse Clara Barton. She was inspired by the global Red Cross network in Europe, which she learned of when visiting after the Civil War. She brought back to the United States the idea of establishing an American Red Cross, and she ultimately served as its leader for twenty-three years.

The organization is a humanitarian effort established to help people (military and civilian) affected by disaster or war. Blood banking is just one of the relief efforts they coordinate. They also offer service in first aid, water safety, public health nursing, hospital and ambulance staffing, safety training, nutrition education, home care for sick or disabled persons, and accident prevention. During times of war or disaster, the American Red Cross's efforts expand to fit the increased need.

Blood banking, though, is one of the American Red Cross's major areas of assistance. During World War II, they collected 13.3 million pints of blood for use in treating wounded servicemen. Today, they supply more than 40 percent of the needed blood and blood products (such as plasma) in the United States.

The improvements made in health care and treatment during the Korean War were many, but a few stand out. One was the establishment of organized blood banks stocked with enough blood and plasma to manage the potential large-scale need that a war would bring about. Blood and plasma were in short supply during parts of World War II, and the United States wanted to ensure that the same thing didn't happen again in another war.

The second major medical development was the use of medevac helicopters as air ambulances to transport the critically wounded off the battlefield and to better health care and treatment facilities. Air transport for the wounded had been used to some extent in World War II and even in World War I, but medevac helicopters were used extensively during the Korean War, and thousands of lives were thought to be saved due to their use.

Finally, there was the establishment of MASH units. MASH stood for mobile army surgical hospital. These were essentially makeshift hospitals set up in combat areas, fully staffed and operational, to treat critical injuries sustained in battle. Much like medevac helicopters, MASH units saved thousands of lives of wounded soldiers who would not have survived without immediate specialized, trained medical care.

During World War II, American forces began to use transport planes to carry wounded soldiers to better health care facilities.

A Development That Sparked a Television Hit

MASH units first appeared late in World War II, but they really became used and known during the Korean War. From this new environment arose entertainment. In 1968, *MASH: A Novel about Three Army Doctors* was published. It centered around a fictional MASH unit during the Korean War. Coauthor H. Richard Hornberger (pen name Richard Hooker) based the novel on his experiences as a physician for the 8055th MASH unit during the Korean War.

The novel was a success, and it inspired a 1970 film called *M*A*S*H*. The film, which starred Donald Sutherland, Tom Skerritt, and Elliott Gould, was wildly successful and earned five Academy Award nominations. In turn, this inspired a television series also entitled *M*A*S*H*, which ran from 1972 to 1983 and, after a struggling first season, was extremely popular. The series finale for *M*A*S*H* remains the most watched series finale in American television history.

Although the novel was based on the author's experiences in the Korean War and both the movie and the television series were set during the Korean War, some events portrayed bore resemblance to events in the Vietnam War. The Vietnam War was going on when the movie and the beginning of the television series were being filmed, and likely the currency of that conflict was why the writers chose to draw some parallels in the movie and the series.

The television series *M*A*S*H* still airs in reruns, and it remains a critical and fan favorite. *TV Guide* named it number twenty-five of their fifty greatest shows of all time in 2002, and the Writers Guild of America called it the fifth best written television series of all time. The series was also nominated for more than one hundred Emmys and ultimately won fourteen.

Bazookas

Finally, on the offensive side, the M20 Super Bazooka rocket launcher was a major development in the Korean War. The bazooka had been invented during World War II, but it was flawed and not terribly effective against armored tanks. The design and technology were examined and refined, resulting in a far superior weapon that the UN forces were able to use to stop the tanks of the invading North Korean armies.

INNOVATION INFORMS WAR

Were it not for the advances in technology that brought us organized blood and plasma banking, medevac helicopters, MASH units, flak vests, and improved rocket launchers, the Korean War might have been a much, much bloodier battle with many more casualties. It's hard to imagine what the scale of the war might have been had these innovations not occurred.

The M20 Super Bazooka was the United States' way of keeping up with the deadlier and more effective weapons being used by opposing forces.

CHAPTER THREE

The Super Bazooka

In war, technology is constantly developing. The Revolutionary War was fought with muskets, bayonets, cannons, rifles, and a variety of swords and knives. Later, the Civil War introduced the use of early grenades and machine guns. World War I included these and introduced the use of aircraft, tanks, and poisonous gas. World War II further developed these weapons and introduced submachine guns, along with the devastating atomic bomb.

When the Korean War came along, all of the tools of World War II, which had ended not even a decade earlier, were still at the military's disposal. But as opposing forces developed deadlier and more effective weapons, the United States needed to keep up. Their answer? The M20 Super Bazooka.

THE BEGINNINGS OF THE BAZOOKA

"Bazooka" is a rather unusual name for a handheld rocket launcher. The original bazookas were also referred to as "stovepipes," but the name "bazooka" has hung on in popular language.

The original bazooka was the M1 rocket launcher, and it was developed during World War II by Edward Uhl, an engineer serving in the army. It was an American invention, but when the Germans got hold of a few of them, they quickly studied their composition and created their own version.

The M1 was an excellent tool for the US Army in World War II, and it saw much use. However, as with any new invention, there were flaws in the original bazooka design. Subsequent versions of the rocket launcher fixed those flaws and eventually led to a more powerful weapon.

DESIGN WEAKNESSES

Although effective, the original bazooka design had some negatives. One problem was that in cold weather, a large smoke trail could be seen from the back of the bazooka after firing, which didn't exactly make for good covert operations.

In addition, the bazooka was quite large, meaning that the person firing it couldn't do so from a small, cramped, protected area. Rather, the shooter had to be out in the open, with room to move, to get a clear line of fire.

And although the bazooka was powerful, its 2.36-inch (60-millimeter) diameter wasn't large enough to house a

Edward Uhl: Father of the Bazooka

The original bazooka was invented during World War II by a US Army lieutenant colonel named Edward Uhl. Uhl had an engineering and military background, having graduated from Lehigh University on an ROTC scholarship. At Lehigh, he had majored in engineering physics.

While serving in the US Army from 1941 to 1947, Uhl and another colonel, Leslie A. Skinner, conceptualized the first bazooka. The unusual name of the weapon came from an improvised tube-shaped musical instrument that a comedian of the time, Bob Burns, had played.

Uhl's goal in creating the bazooka was to invent a weapon that would deliver a powerful rocket blast without the burning powder injuring the operator's face. Uhl said he was inspired by a 5-foot (1.5-meter) tube he saw in a scrap pile one day. It was roughly the same size as the rocket they were looking to launch: "I said, 'That's the answer! Put the tube on a soldier's shoulder with a rocket inside and away it goes.'"

The bazooka was an instant success. A general tested a prototype in 1942, and when he hit his target, the army eagerly ordered five thousand launchers and twenty-five thousand rockets. The bazooka could penetrate more than 4 inches (10 centimeters) of tank armor.

After the war, Uhl continued to work in the weapons and aerospace industry, perhaps most notably as head of the prominent aerospace company Fairchild Industries, Inc. Uhl died in 2010 at the age of ninety-two.

substantial rocket to bring down a German tank. Those firing the bazooka had to aim carefully at less protected areas of a tank to get a successful hit; otherwise, it was a bit like David throwing small rocks at the giant Goliath!

The original bazooka was always a rather finicky weapon, susceptible to temperature extremes and unfavorable conditions. Its reliability was questionable in very cold or tropical climates, as well as in sandy or dusty conditions.

Despite its weaknesses, the original bazooka *was* a useful and powerful weapon, and in fact, General Dwight D. Eisenhower referred to it as one of the four factors that helped the Allies win World War II: "The bazooka, the Jeep, the atom bomb, and the C-47 Gooney Bird."

THE NEW-AND-IMPROVED M20 SUPER BAZOOKA

The Germans had gotten hold of a few bazookas during World War II and had reverse engineered their own version, which became known as the *Panzerschreck*. It was basically a bigger, better bazooka, with its 3.46-inch (88 mm) diameter, compared to the bazooka's 2.36 inches (60 mm).

Upon seeing the improvements in the weapon, the United States redesigned the bazooka after World War II ended. Not content to match the *Panzerschreck*'s 3.46-inch diameter, the redesigned M20 Super Bazooka featured a 3.54-inch (90 mm) diameter. The rockets fired from the M20 had better penetrating capability than those fired from the *Panzerschreck* and a better effective range. At about 12 pounds (5.4 kilograms), the M20 was also much lighter than the 20-pound (9 kg) *Panzerschreck* and comparable in weight to the original M1A1 rocket launcher, which weighed in at just under 13 pounds (6 kg). The rockets for any launcher naturally added some weight, but the fact that the empty weapon was lighter than the *Panzerschreck* was a plus.

While the original bazooka could only penetrate about 4 inches (10 cm) of tank armor, the M20 Super Bazooka offered vastly improved penetration. The shaped rockets fired from the M20 ensured a concentrated force of explosion on a small surface area of the tank, which meant the penetration was deeper—reportedly up to 11 inches (28 cm)! Further, the M20 Super Bazooka offered a slightly improved range. The bazookas used in World War II had a range of up to about 700 yards (640 m), but the M20 Super Bazooka had a range of up to about 950 yards (870 m).

The M20 redesign also offered more firing options. No longer did soldiers have to go completely out in the open to fire the weapon, which many had seen as a suicide mission. With the redesigned M20, the Super Bazooka could be fired from sitting, standing, and kneeling positions. Moreover, the tubes that made up the bazooka could be broken down for easier carrying when soldiers were on the move.

The ammunition for the M20 was also improved upon. Part of the temperature sensitivity of the original bazookas had to do with the sensitivity of the rockets. For the M20, ammunition was packaged in a moisture-resistant pack, and soldiers were given instructions on how to store the ammo in the correct conditions and how to properly lubricate the M20 launcher.

In theory, the new-and-improved Super Bazooka would be an excellent tool for the UN forces fighting in South Korea. However, difficulties loomed in the form of budget cuts. There had been significant cuts in military spending after the end of World War II, and when the Korean War began, the military was initially equipped with older models of bazooka and older ammunition. Not only did these tools fail to be terribly effective, suffering from the same issues that had plagued them during World War II, but the military found that the ammunition had actually deteriorated during its years of storage and thus didn't always detonate properly.

On June 25, 1950, when the Korean People's Army invaded South Korea, the US Army stationed in the region numbered about six hundred. They were no match for the thousands of North Korean soldiers who arrived in tanks—their World War II–era bazookas fired ammunition that more or less bounced off the armor of the incoming tanks.

Sergeant Bill McCarthy, who was a member of Task Force Smith in the Korean War—the first ground maneuver unit of the US Army to enter combat—was aghast at the inefficiency of the weapons the US forces were equipped with. He reportedly sent a telegram to President Ronald Reagan in 1985, remembering the inefficacy of the bazookas the troops were initially supplied in Korea. Sgt. McCarthy feared the same issue would plague US military defense again and wanted President Reagan to be aware of how the outdated technology had crippled the task force in their attempts to hold off a 1950 North Korean attack. The lack of adequate weapons had a profound effect on the very early battles in the Korean War.

Within about two weeks, the Twenty-Fourth Infantry Division, stationed in South Korea, had been outfitted with the new M20 Super Bazookas, which were rushed through production. Indeed, once the military realized the problem in using the old ammunition and launchers and sent M20s and the associated M28A2 **HEAT rocket** ammunition to the troops in South Korea, the problem was resolved. The UN forces quickly found that the new-and-improved Super Bazooka could destroy the North Korean tanks. On its first day used in battle, the Super Bazooka reportedly claimed eight North Korean tanks.

THE IMPACT OF THE M20

A weapon is only as effective as the soldiers who use it, but certainly putting the improved M20 Super Bazooka into the hands of UN forces changed the tone of the Korean War. Now the forces in South Korea could fight back; now it was a fair fight. No longer would the forces fighting in South Korea be overrun by incoming tanks from North Korea. With the introduction of the M20 Super Bazooka, the forces in South Korea could defend themselves.

Improved flak vests protected troops during the Korean War.

CHAPTER FOUR

The Flak Vest

Certainly, offense is a key principle of war. Wars cannot be won by a particular side if they take no forward offensive action. A good defense may allow them to hold off the enemy, but it's not a winning strategy. In fact, the strategic offensive principle of war suggests that strong offensive action is the way to achieve a strategic advantage.

With that said, the importance of good defense cannot be ignored. Part of a good defense is protecting the soldiers who are fighting for your side. Armies do that with strategy, but they also do it with a deceptively simple tool: body armor. The only problem is, some body armor is so cumbersome that it becomes a hindrance during battle. During the Korean War, significant advancements in body armor were made that allowed soldiers to more comfortably protect their bodies on the battlefield.

A BRIEF HISTORY

Body armor has been used in battle for centuries. The ancient Greeks in the Mycenaean Age (roughly 1600–1100 BCE), for example, were thought to be the first to wear metal armor. Spartan soldiers in the era of 431 to 404 BCE wore metal helmets, chest plates (sometimes referred to as tunics), and shin guards, and they carried metal shields. Roman soldiers during the Roman Empire wore body armor as well. Japanese samurai warriors wore iron-plated armor starting as early as the seventh century CE. In the Middle Ages (roughly the fifth to the fifteenth century CE), European knights wore chain mail and plate armor both for protection and to show their valor and standing on the battlefield.

These various types of armor were effective at protecting the soldier from some types of attack, such as knife and sword strikes, but they weren't without their weaknesses. First, this armor wasn't immune to gunfire. In fact, British soldiers in World War I found that the body armor of that era actually made them *more* susceptible to bodily harm by gunfire, as the curved metal chest plates tended to guide bullets toward their body. Second, armor was incredibly heavy and in many cases, cumbersome. It was difficult to move quickly and to maneuver in small spaces if you were covered by a suit of metal armor.

By the time of the Civil War, the United States was on its way to solving one of the two problems. Rudimentary bulletproof

The body armor worn by medieval knights wasn't terribly practical, or comfortable!

vests were available. However, they weren't issued by the military—instead, soldiers could buy them from private vendors if they chose. Two companies out of New Haven, Connecticut, manufactured the vests, and both versions basically consisted of cast-iron plates.

However, the vests weren't widely used. For one, the soldiers purchasing and wearing the vests tended to be ridiculed by fellow soldiers who chose not to. Second and probably more to the point, the manufacturers hadn't solved the second problem that existed with body armor: the vests were bulletproof, but they were still incredibly heavy.

By World War I, the United States was experimenting with creating a lighter-weight form of body armor, but they hadn't been terribly successful. The body armor of World War I weighed roughly 40 pounds (18 kg). That weight was still prohibitive for troops, so body armor was not used much during the war.

Nevertheless, the United States kept working on it, and during World War II, they introduced the first flak jacket. The name came from a contraction of the German word *Fliegerabwehrkanone,* a type of antiaircraft gun and one of the many types of explosives that the vests were meant to protect against. Flak jackets were first used by aircrews and were meant to protect the crews from flying shrapnel. However, development teams still struggled to minimize the jacket's weight and comfort. By that point, the bulletproof vests and jackets weighed around 22 pounds (10 kg). Although they were issued to troops on the ground as well as in the air, many ground troops refused to wear them. By the end of World War II, flak vests and body armor still weren't widely used—they were just too heavy to be a helpful protection tool for soldiers.

Korean War–Era Flak Vests

When the Korean War broke out, the need for better body armor had not been forgotten. In fact, since around 1943, in conjunction with the Army Quartermaster Corps, Dow Chemical Company had been working on a material for flak vests that combined fiberglass with resin under high pressure. This created a glass fiber laminate. Dow called the material Doron, after Brigadier General Georges F. Doriot, who was the head of the project. The Doron vests weighed just over 10 pounds (4.5 kg), and they satisfied the Quartermaster Corps' wish for a form of nonmetal body armor.

Around the same time (late and post–World War II), the Army Ordnance Corps was working on the M12 vest, which weighed just over 12 pounds (5 kg) and was made of aluminum plates and nylon fabric. These vests were used at the outset of the Korean War, but later in the war, American troops wore primarily Doron vests or all-nylon vests, and the M12 vests were worn by the Republic of Korea troops.

The Quartermaster Corps hadn't given up on Doron, even though they were also experimenting with all-nylon vests. In fact, both the US Navy and the US Marines were interested in using Doron in their body armor. In 1951, one hundred hybrid Doron-nylon vests were shipped to Korea for testing purposes, and based on the test results, the US Marines adopted the vest for their use.

The Father of Doron

Georges Frederic Doriot was born in France to Auguste Doriot, an automotive pioneer, and his wife, Berthe Camille Baehler. After joining the French army, Georges later moved to the United States to pursue an MBA at the Massachusetts Institute of Technology (MIT). Instead, he found himself at Harvard Business School, and despite never completing his MBA, he became a professor and assistant dean at the school, as well as a venture capitalist, founding the earliest public venture capital firm in the United States, American Research and Development Corporation (ARDC), in 1946.

Georges became a United States citizen at the age of forty-one, in 1940. The next year, he became a lieutenant colonel in the Quartermaster Corps, where he was the director of the Military Planning Division. While there, he oversaw Dow Chemical's development of Doron, which was later used in flak vests for the US Marines. He was promoted to brigadier general and retired from the army in 1945 with a Distinguished Service Medal. He has also been honored with the French Legion of Honor and as a Commander of the British Empire.

In addition to overseeing the Doron project, Doriot was instrumental in the development of cold-weather socks, sunscreen, insecticide, Saran Wrap, and **K rations**.

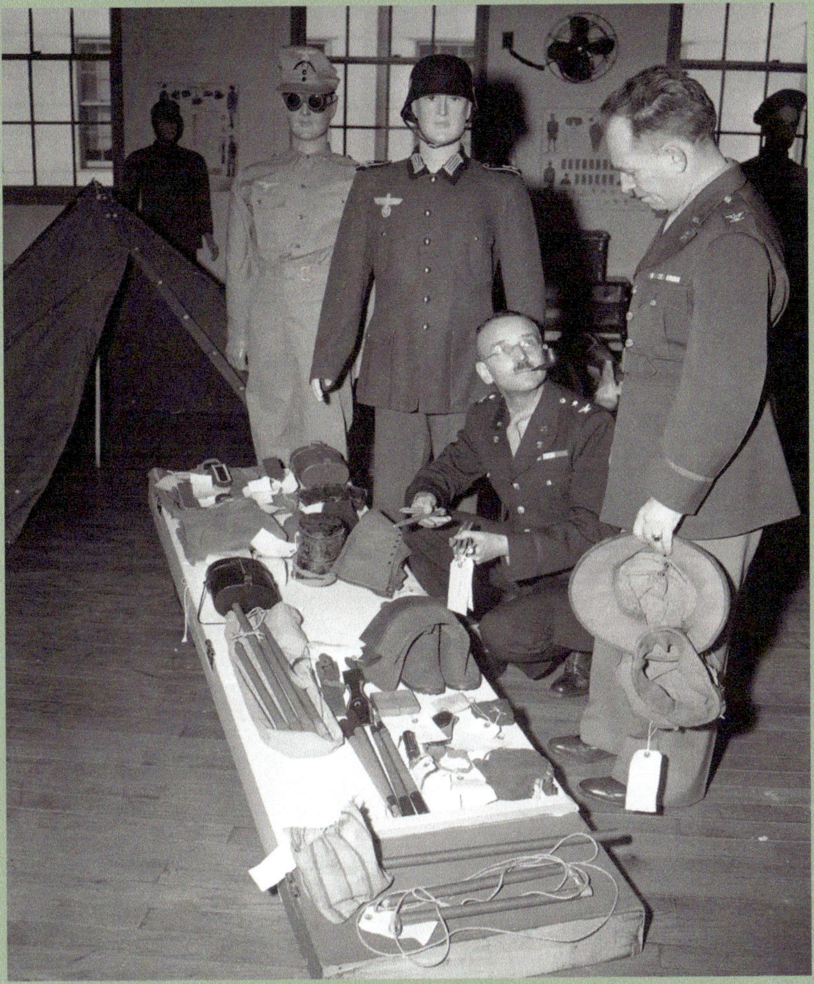

Georges Frederic Doriot (*kneeling*), the father of Doron, poses with weapons taken from captured German soldiers during World War II.

The all-nylon vests were created by the Quartermaster Corps after the Ordnance Corps reported that nylon was the best lightweight flexible ballistic material. Surprisingly, ballistics tests showed that nylon was even better than steel at stopping missile fragments from penetrating a soldier's body. By 1950, the Quartermaster Corps had created a one-piece nylon flak vest that still serves as the basic model for today's body armor vests. The US Army preferred the all-nylon vests to the Doron vests and requested that the vests be field-tested for ultimate adoption by the army. They were indeed tested, with favorable results. According to a fact sheet issued from the Office of the Quartermaster General in 1952, they appeared to deflect "approximately 65 percent of all types of missiles, 75 percent of all fragments, and 25 percent of all small-arms fire." In addition, the Office of the Quartermaster reported that the nylon vests "reduced torso wounds by 60 to 70 percent" and reduced the severity of wounds inflicted "by 25 to 35 percent." However, the vests were not mass-produced and thus could not be quickly shipped to troops, so the Doron vests worn by the Marines were often used instead, despite the promising field results from tests of the all-nylon army vests.

Neither of these vests was 100 percent bulletproof, but both could significantly reduce the number of mortal injuries suffered by soldiers hit by **mortar** or artillery fire, or by shrapnel or grenade fragments. The Quartermaster Corps' 1952 fact sheet called both types of vests "extremely effective in reducing combat casualties."

THE IMPACT OF THE IMPROVED FLAK VEST

The exact number of casualties from the Korean War is unknown, but most sources list the number of deaths of American troops as somewhere around forty thousand. That number undoubtedly would've been much higher if it weren't for the advances made in body armor and the introduction of lighter-weight flak vests that could easily be worn in combat. Today, body armor continues to evolve, but certainly the gains made during development for the Korean War saved countless lives and reduced injuries in those who were hurt.

This modern-day soldier wears a flak vest during a field exercise.

Medevac helicopters were one of many advances in health care made during the Korean War.

CHAPTER FIVE

Advances in Medicine

War does not come without injury and casualties. It's a sad but true fact that many soldiers will be injured—sometimes critically—in combat and on the battlefield. With every war, though, advancements in medical care have helped save lives. The Korean War, in particular, offered several significant medical advancements that helped with the care of the wounded.

BLOOD BANKING

Although Dr. Charles Drew had pioneered plasma storage during World War II, when the Korean War started, the United States did not yet have an organized blood-banking system for the military. They had plans for a system, but the plans had not been implemented. Naturally, this was problematic—particularly in the early part of the war, when North Korean forces were making considerable gains in the south. The military knew how to collect, store, and transfuse blood, but they didn't have an established blood bank. Even before the war broke out, they knew that was a problem. In 1949, the newly appointed director of medical services for the Office of the Secretary of Defense recognized that the United States didn't have enough whole blood or plasma stored in the event of an emergency, such as wartime. He appointed a task force to study the issue and explore solutions. The resultant report was submitted to the secretary of defense in early 1950 and became Department of Defense policy shortly before the war broke out.

Among other things, the report included recommendations for the amount of whole blood and plasma that should be banked for wartime. Also, because the task group didn't think the Department of Defense could rapidly establish the needed blood bank, it recommended collaboration with various Armed Forces blood banks; commercial civilian blood banks; and the American Red Cross, which had an established blood-collection program used by civilian hospitals in the United States.

The task force further recommended standardizing collection and storage procedures among these agencies, with legislation that any blood collected and stored meet certain biological standards. Moreover, they suggested that a war reserve be created even during peacetime so that the United States would not face a blood shortage in a time of war.

As with any sort of new policy, there was dissension in the ranks and disagreement about some of the finer points of the task force's recommendations. However, in August 1950, the secretary of defense awarded responsibility for the blood program to Dr. Richard L. Meiling, the director of medical services at the Department of Defense, and ordered that the director of medical services should ensure implementation of the program.

The program underwent reorganizations and changes during the war, but ultimately, with the help of the American Red Cross and other cooperating blood banks the national blood program operated successfully throughout the Korean War, saving the lives of countless wounded servicemen.

MEDEVAC HELICOPTERS

Injured and deceased soldiers have been transported by aircraft since at least 1870, when soldiers were transported out of war-torn Paris by hot-air balloon during the Franco-Prussian War. Soldiers were lifted by "air ambulance" during World War I, but aircraft were in their early days then, so transports were few and far between. In World War II, aircraft were much more commonplace, and the first documented medical transport by helicopter occurred when a US Army helicopter was used to transport wounded British soldiers out of Burma. Still, medical transport by helicopter wasn't commonplace.

That is, until the Korean War. Helicopters became much more used by the military during that time, and one of their uses was for medevac, short for "medical evacuation." In some cases,

The Father of Blood Banking

Charles Drew

Although blood banking was systematically organized during the Korean War, it began about a decade earlier, when a young, gifted African American doctor named Charles Richard Drew, working under a fellowship, helped Dr. John Scudder set up an experimental blood bank. Drew had long been interested in transfusion medicine and had wanted to study transfusion therapy at the Mayo Clinic, but racial prejudice prevented him from realizing that dream.

Racial prejudice reared its head again when Drew won a fellowship to Presbyterian Hospital in New York under a well-known surgeon. The surgeon, Allen Whipple, assigned Drew to work on the blood bank project rather than following the usual path of gaining surgical experience—which ensured that African American Drew would not have direct contact with patients.

As disappointing as the blatant racism was, it turned out to be a positive for Drew. Scudder was amazed at Drew's natural talent, and even Whipple grew to be impressed by the brilliant young doctor. Drew threw his energies into the blood-banking project and used his work there to inform his thesis, "Banked Blood: A Study in Blood Preservation," which earned him a doctorate from Columbia University—the first African American to earn the prestigious degree from that university.

So brilliant was Drew's research that he later earned a position as the head of the Blood for Britain Project, which aimed to get much-needed blood and plasma to the struggling British soldiers, who were under German attack. Drew's exacting standards allowed his team to successfully transport plasma to England. By the time the Blood for Britain Project ended, they had collected more than fourteen thousand blood donations and shipped more than 1,320 gallons (5,000 liters) of plasma saline solution to the United Kingdom.

The Blood for Britain Project was the predecessor of the Red Cross's program to mass-produce dried plasma, of which Drew was the assistant director. Drew also masterminded mobile blood-donation trucks with refrigerators, also known as bloodmobiles, which are still used today.

In a rather cruel irony, although Drew was the assistant director of the program and the brain behind the original concept, because of his race he would've been ineligible to participate in it. At that time, the American Red Cross refused donations from African Americans. They later changed their policy, but they insisted on segregating the blood so that Caucasians would only receive blood donated by Caucasians, and African Americans would only receive African American blood. Despite his work with the organization, Drew was openly critical of what he called their "unscientific and insulting" practice.

Drew actually did not live to see the Korean War; he died just months before it broke out, as a result of severe injuries suffered in a car accident. But were it not for Drew's pioneering work, the further refined blood-banking process that saved so many lives in the Korean War likely would not have existed.

the medical evacuation was actually a transport of a dead body. However, the military quickly realized that these helicopters could also be used to transport stabilized but critical patients from treatment areas on the battlefield to more advanced treatment facilities.

The first medical evacuation by helicopter during the Korean War happened in August 1950, not long after the outbreak of war. A Bell 47 helicopter flew wounded soldiers off the battlefield after securing them in basket stretchers attached to the landing feet of the helicopter. Not a pleasurable way to travel, for sure—but the other option was perhaps death.

Conditions were rough. The wounded soldiers were subject to cold air temperatures and wound contamination, which the transport teams tried to fight by covering them with blankets. It was a crude system at best, but it worked. More than twenty thousand injured soldiers were carried out of the battlefield by medevac helicopters. And whereas in World War II the rate of deaths per casualties was 4.5:100, during the Korean War that rate dropped to 2.5:100. Certainly, there may have been additional factors at play, such as advances in medical treatment, but it is widely believed that using medevac helicopters to transport patients quickly to more advanced medical facilities was a major factor in lowering the death rate among battlefield casualties.

Although the Bell 47 was the first helicopter used for a medevac flight during the Korean War, it wasn't the only helicopter used for that purpose. The Sikorsky S-51 also operated as an air ambulance, as did the Bell H-13. In both helicopters, space was at a premium. The helicopters could fit two crewmembers and just one injured soldier. If the soldier was transported inside the **fuselage** of the helicopter, his legs stuck out the side of the helicopter because room was so tight.

Neither of these helicopters was particularly well equipped for long-haul flights, but that wasn't a problem during the Korean War. The battle lines, particularly during the latter half of the war, tended to be around the 38th parallel, and there were nearby MASH units where pilots could fly the wounded. Later, the military would need transport helicopters capable of going longer distances, but during the Korean War, the Bell 47 and Sikorsky S-51 could handle the transports just fine.

The medevac helicopters were invaluable for transport, saving tens of thousands of lives, but naturally, they had to have someplace to transport critical patients. That place was often a MASH unit.

MASH UNITS

An incredibly popular television series of the 1970s and early 1980s was *M*A*S*H,* based on a 1970 film of the same name—which itself was based on a 1968 novel. In fact, the television series was so popular that it remains one of the highest-rated programs in US television history. The novel, the movie, and the book were all about a fictional MASH unit during the Korean War.

MASH stands for mobile army surgical hospital and describes a hospital established in a combat area. Like several other technologies that took shape during the Korean War, MASH units actually came about late in World War II, but they were much more extensively used during the Korean War. MASH units were so successful in military medical treatment that they existed until 2006, during Operation Iraqi Freedom, when they were replaced by combat support hospitals, which are essentially the same thing with a less catchy acronym to describe them.

The idea behind MASH units was that soldiers injured on the battlefield needed professional medical care as soon as possible—and that meant in the combat zone. If the injured had to wait for transport to get access to necessary medical care, it might be too late—or, if they did survive, their treatment might not be as successful. Timing is a critical component in emergency medical care, and MASH units allowed medical staff treating injured soldiers to have time on their side. The first MASH unit to arrive in Korea was the 8063rd, but it was quickly followed by others. Patient capacity at the units could be more than two hundred beds.

There was a triage system in place, of course. However, not every soldier wounded on the battlefield needed immediate extensive medical care. Those with less serious injuries could be treated through general first aid. For soldiers requiring immediate surgery to stabilize them for further treatment, there were battalion aid stations. Due to the severity of injuries seen at the battalion aid stations, deaths were not unheard of. However, if a patient survived the battalion aid station and was moved to the MASH unit, that patient had a 97 percent chance of surviving his injuries.

In their history of MASH units, published in the *Journal of the National Medical Association*, Major Booker King, MD, FACS, and Colonel Ismail Jatoi, MD, PhD, FACS, declare MASH units "one of the defining aspects of the Korean War." The MASH units resulted in "improvements in resuscitation and trauma care, patient transport, blood storage and distribution, patient triage, and evacuation." In short, the use of MASH units had a major positive impact on almost every facet of combat-zone medical care.

THE IMPACT OF MEDICAL ADVANCEMENTS

Between organized blood banking, medevac helicopters, and MASH units, the impact of medical advancements during the Korean War cannot be overstated. The mortality rates of the Korean War compared to the earlier World War I and World War II are evidence as well. In World War I, the mortality rate for injured soldiers was 8.5 percent. That rate dropped to 4 percent during World War II, but it dropped even further, to 2.5 percent, during the Korean War. No doubt thousands of lives were saved thanks to advances in medical treatment and transport.

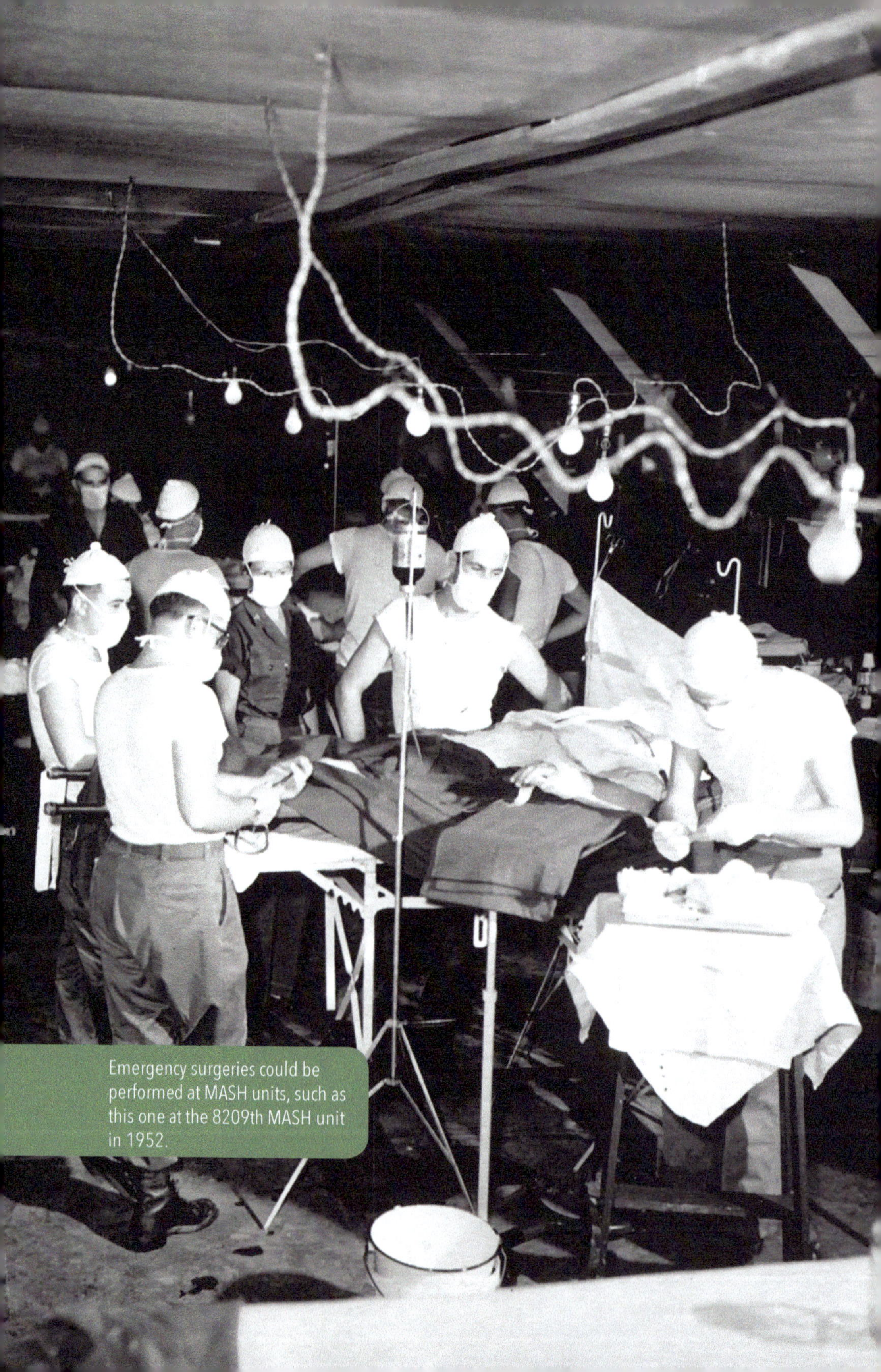

Emergency surgeries could be performed at MASH units, such as this one at the 8209th MASH unit in 1952.

CHAPTER SIX

Technology's Effects During the Korean War

The effects of technology development are both immediate and long lasting. During the Korean War, improvements were made to weapons technology (in particular, refinements to the bazooka), safety technology (in the form of flak vests), and medical technology (with MASH units being installed, coordinated blood banks being set up, and helicopters being used as evacuation air ambulances). All of these advances had long-term impacts: weapons similar to the bazooka are still used today, body armor continues to be used in both military and civilian installments, and medevac helicopters and blood banks are even more widely used than they were during the Korean War. Even MASH units still exist, though they are much greater in scope and are now referred to as combat support hospitals (CSHs). But what about the immediate effects of these technologies? How did they change the face of the Korean War? And how did they affect society as a whole?

TANK STOPPER: THE M20 SUPER BAZOOKA

The whole point of bazookas was to stop tanks. They were designed specifically as antitank rocket launchers. The problem was, however, that early bazookas couldn't really stop tanks. Not well, anyway. They could if the ammunition hit its target in a weak spot—generally in the lower or top armor—but they weren't very effective if they hit the areas of a tank covered in heavier armor. Because bazookas were a shoulder-held weapon, generally the men firing them were firing straight on at tanks—not at the lower-belly portion or the top.

Thus, early bazookas were only somewhat effective. It was kind of like that scene in *Star Wars* where Luke Skywalker has to fire from his X-Wing fighter into the *exact* single weak spot of the massive Death Star to destroy it. If he succeeds in hitting that tiny weak target, great! The Death Star is destroyed, and the Jedi can go back to a victory celebration at home. But if he misses—well, his bullets have done little more than bounce off the massive structure.

The M20 Super Bazooka changed that for the Korean War. Not only did it have greater penetration capability, but it also had greater distance accuracy. It had an improved gunsight that helped soldiers fire it with greater accuracy from farther distances.

The M20 Super Bazooka improved US forces' ability to disable or destroy enemy tanks during the Korean War.

It also fired shaped-charge HEAT rockets, which concentrated the resulting explosion on a small area of the tank for greater penetration and destruction.

The M20 also allowed for more flexibility in shooting than previous bazookas had. It could be fired from sitting, standing, or kneeling positions, which gave soldiers more flexibility on how they could aim and fire on tanks.

The M20 was known to be particularly effective against Soviet T-34 tanks. This is notable because the North Korean armies were equipped with T-34 tanks when they invaded South Korea in 1950. Because the South Korean forces and the US troops were initially outfitted with older-model bazookas and weapons, it's not surprising that in the initial invasion, the South Koreans were no match for the advancing North Korean tanks. Once the US forces in South Korea received their shipment of M20 Super Bazookas, however, the tone of the fight changed. No longer could the North Korean forces simply steamroll over them. Now, the US and South Koreans could fight back.

Without the M20 Super Bazooka in their arsenal, it's questionable what the outcome of the Korean War would've been. As it was, there was no real winner to the conflict—North Korea and South Korea are still separate entities today, and their relationship is not exactly the most peaceful. However, it's entirely possible that if the United States and associated forces in South Korea had *not* had access to the M20 Super Bazooka, the North

Korean forces could've made a lot more progress than they did, perhaps ultimately realizing their goal of taking over South Korea.

SHRAPNEL STOPPER: THE FLAK VEST

While the M20 Super Bazooka was an offensive and defensive weapon, the flak vest was simply a defensive tool. It existed solely to reduce the number of war casualties and to protect the soldiers who wore it.

Body armor had existed for centuries in various forms, but it often wasn't worn because it was incredibly heavy, cumbersome, and uncomfortable. Plus, it didn't tend to provide much protection against bullets. That changed during the Korean War. Two types of technology (Doron and nylon flak vests) resulted in a form of body armor that was both lighter and more resistant to ammunition. That's not to say it was *entirely* resistant to ammunition. The flak vests developed for and used in Korea were fairly good at stopping shrapnel and other fragments from penetrating a soldier's flesh, but they didn't tend to be very effective at stopping bullets from small-arms fire.

Still, it was better than nothing. The use of grenades, mortars, and other artillery fired from rocket launchers meant that shrapnel and debris was a very real concern to soldiers. Certainly, bullets were always a concern, but shrapnel and debris were no less a concern. So the fact that flak vests could provide protection from airborne debris was a plus. The fact flak vests were actually

Improvements to flak vests continued, leading to more soldiers wearing them in future conflicts, such as the Vietnam War.

somewhat wearable (if still rather uncomfortable) was another plus. According to Jack Lewis, the author of *The Gun Digest Book of Assualt Weapons,* ninety thousand flak vests were used in combat during the Korean War.

No doubt, body armor saved lives. It's reported that the army found that flak vests used during the Korean War reduced wounds to the chest, back, and abdomen by up to 70 percent. One soldier recalled that the flak vest he wore "undoubtedly saved my life, because I had fragments in both my arms and both my legs up to the tops of my thighs but nothing penetrated my stomach or chest areas." He also speaks of a fellow patient in the MASH unit who was hit by a Chinese **burp gun**: "He had one bullet in his left arm, one in his right arm and a row of bruises across his chest, so clearly in his case the flak vest worked even better than for me!"

Although it's impossible to determine exactly how many lives flak vests saved during the Korean War, the numbers indicate that overall, the death toll from the war was improved over earlier wars. The mortality rate for injured soldiers during the Korean War was 2.5 percent, where it had been 4 percent during World War II. Certainly, advancements in medical care likely contributed to the drop in mortality rate, but it's likely that the safety provided by flak vests was also a factor in protecting soldiers' lives.

CASUALTY STOPPER: MEDICAL ADVANCEMENTS

There will never be a way to have a war without casualties. It is simply the nature of war that people die for the cause. Lives are lost and families are torn apart, and the only hope is that the sacrifice is for a greater good. But certainly, the goal is to minimize the loss of life in a conflict. The United States doesn't view its soldiers as simply throwaways whose lives don't matter; they are committed to preserving the lives of as many soldiers as possible. This was evident recently in the military's efforts to bring home prisoner-of-war Bowe Bergdahl from the Middle East. After Bergdahl spent five years held by the Taliban in captivity, the United States might have simply written off the life of one soldier, but instead they remained committed to bringing him home—no one left behind. The goal was no different in Korea—the military wanted to preserve the lives of as many soldiers as possible, so having prompt, quality medical care was a must.

Establishing MASH units was a huge step in achieving this goal. With MASH units in combat zones, soldiers could be treated immediately after being injured. Many treated in MASH units had injuries severe enough that attempting to transport them to another location for treatment would've resulted in death. Being able to perform emergency life-saving surgery on site was a game changer.

It's impossible to say how many lives were saved by MASH units, but Brian Fitzgerald, author of *The Korean War: America's Forgotten War*, calls it "thousands," and according to *An Encyclopedia of American Women at War*, 97 percent of wounded soldiers treated in MASH units ultimately survived. Furthermore, according to Edward Dailey, author of *MacArthur's X Corps in*

Korea: Ischon to the Yalu 1950, MASH units were the key to lowering mortality rates.

Blood banking, too, was a key in saving lives during this conflict. Blood transfusions had existed since long before the war, but banking blood to have on hand during times of combat was not formalized until the Korean War. Once Dr. Charles Drew

Blood banks, such as this one in 1951 in Denver, Colorado, collected blood and plasma for life-saving transfusions during the Korean War.

pioneered his methods for blood banking and plasma storage during World War II, the US military was able to collaborate with the American Red Cross and other organizations to establish formal blood banks to ensure that blood and plasma were available for wounded soldiers in need of transfusions.

According to the Armed Services Blood Program, the blood-banking and transfusion program was enormously successful during the Korean War. The military focused on using Type O– blood because it could be transfused to any soldier—there was no need to wait for blood-type matching. They reported that in 1952, they administered fifty thousand blood transfusions, and only four of those resulted in major **hemolytic** reactions that caused acute kidney failure. Those four were reportedly all from blood obtained locally, not blood that had been banked in the United States and sent overseas.

As with MASH units, it's impossible to know how many lives blood banking during the Korean War saved, but it's easy to see that the impact was great. On-site treatment at MASH units plus the availability of blood for transfusions saved a lot of lives that might otherwise have been lost.

The final major medical development of the Korean War that saved countless lives was the use of medevac helicopters. While some injuries could be handled strictly at a MASH unit, other injuries were serious enough that the patient needed to be stabilized at a MASH unit and then transported to a larger medical

Medical air transport saved countless lives during the Korean War.

The Visibility and Controversy of War

The Korean War is sometimes called the Forgotten War because it doesn't get the same attention in history as the two wars it was sandwiched between: World War II and the Vietnam War. In reality, the three wars happened in a relatively compact timespan. and because of that, it's interesting to examine public attitudes toward them.

World War II was largely seen as a necessary war. In general, Americans supported it. The death toll was tremendous and many families were splintered, but there was an overall feeling that the men and women serving the United States were doing so with good purpose. The atrocities committed by the Nazis were horrifying, innocent people were being slaughtered in horrible deaths, and Japan posed a very real threat.

Vietnam, on the other hand, was a wildly unpopular war. Certainly, there were Americans who supported it, but there was a huge segment of the population that felt there was no need for the United States to be involved and that American soldiers were dying with no real purpose. People burned draft cards in protest; people fled the country to dodge the draft. The **counterculture** staged visible antiwar protests. That disdain for the war even led to a general disdain and distrust of the government.

And there, sandwiched right in the middle, was the Korean War. It was neither strongly supported nor protested. It simply *was*.

Why the lackluster reaction to the war—either positive or negative? First, the war broke out not long after the end of World War II, so

Americans were still in a general war mindset. The Cold War was a new and frightening threat, so Americans generally supported the idea that a Communist takeover was a threat and a stand should be taken against that. So generally, Americans either supported the war or just didn't see any reason to oppose it. Thus, no protests were necessary.

Moreover, it didn't evoke the same reaction that World War II did. There was no Hitler in the Korean War—no dictator ordering mass genocide of innocent groups of people. The Korean War was about political maneuvering and power, not about human atrocities. So it didn't provoke quite the same response as World War II.

Also, the Korean War was comparatively short. The Vietnam War was incredibly long, and protests didn't start in full force until it had actually been going for quite some time. Basically, the American public grew tired of being involved in a long war that they eventually decided they never should've entered in the first place.

Finally, the media wasn't as present during the Korean War as during the Vietnam War. Vietnam was called the Living Room War because it played out on people's television sets every night, as photojournalism and news footage took the stage. That wasn't the case with the Korean War; it was more out of sight, out of mind.

In any war, there will be supporters and detractors, but the Korean War was a relatively quiet, "forgotten" conflict.

facility for further care—and that's where medevac helicopters came in.

According to Major William G. Howard, the use of medevac helicopters and MASH units "fundamentally changed the Army's medical-evaluation doctrine." It's estimated that there were 20,000 casualties transported by helicopter medevac during the Korean War. One specific pilot logged 824 medical evacuations over a span of ten months. On February 20, 1951, 750 critically wounded soldiers were evacuated, and an Eighth Army surgeon estimated that half of them would have died if medevac transportation had not been available.

Logistically, medevac helicopters were a must. Much of the combat area in Korea consisted of terrain with either primitive or nonexistent roads, so traditional ground transportation was particularly ineffective for patients with critical injuries. A helicopter needed only a flat area to land and take off; roads were unnecessary.

General Douglas MacArthur favored medevac helicopters for transporting the wounded, too. After a meeting with Army Surgeon General Major General Raymond W. Bliss in 1950, MacArthur recommended that medevac helicopters "should be in the Tables of Organization and Equipment and should be part of medical equipment—just as an ambulance is."

OVERALL BENEFITS OF THE TECHNOLOGY OF THE KOREAN WAR

The major technological developments of the Korean War were beneficial from an offensive standpoint as well as a defensive standpoint. Super Bazookas were effective at disabling tanks, which strategically worked both as an offensive strike and as a defensive move. Flak vests reduced the number of mortal injuries to soldiers from shrapnel and other debris. Lastly, the medical advances made immediately prior to and during the war saved the lives of thousands.

Many of these same technological developments came into play in the Vietnam War shortly thereafter as well, extending their benefit beyond just the confines of the Korean War.

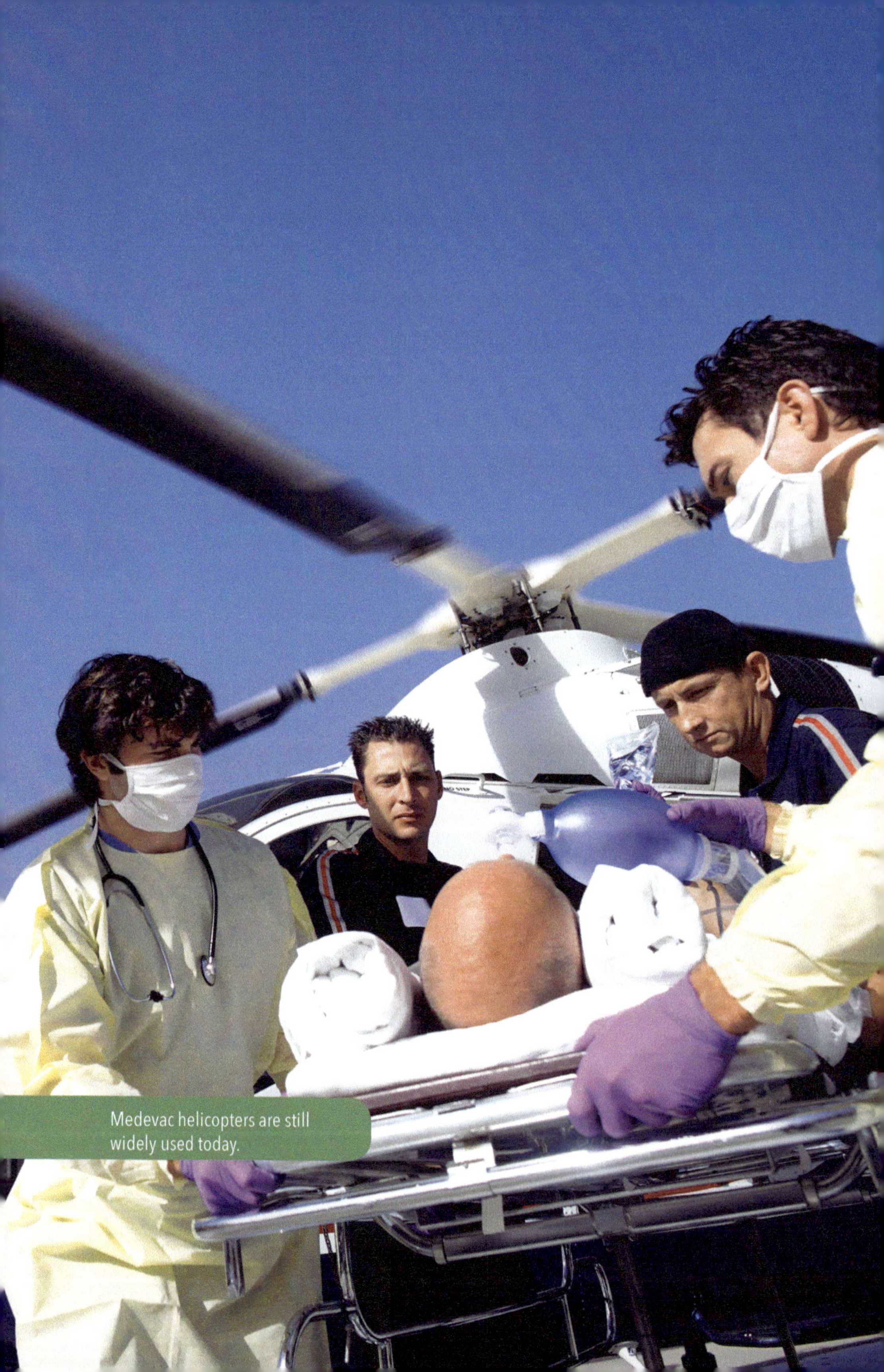

Medevac helicopters are still widely used today.

CHAPTER SEVEN

The Technology Today

As time goes on, technology evolves. What was groundbreaking one day eventually branches off into one of two directions: it becomes obsolete, or it evolves into something even more innovative. In the case of the major innovations of the Korean War, the technology has continued to evolve and improve. Some of the inventions that came out of the Korean War are still used in ways that resemble their 1950s form, but some have changed quite significantly.

BAZOOKAS OF TODAY

The bazooka was the first handheld antitank weapon when it was invented during World War II. It was subsequently improved for use during the Korean War, and the improvements were substantial. Whereas the first bazookas could fire ammunition with only enough force to penetrate about 4 inches (10 cm) of armor, the M20 Super Bazooka developed for use in the Korean War could fire ammunition with enough force to penetrate up to 11 inches (28 cm) of tank armor. Range and ammunition were improved as well.

Subsequent improvements and variations were done on the design of the Super Bazooka, and bazookas were used by the US military during the early part of the Vietnam War. Other countries have used bazookas in combat after the Vietnam War, but the last US military use was during the Vietnam War.

However, there are similar weapons used by the US military today. When the bazooka fell out of use, it was replaced by the 3.54-inch (90 mm) shoulder-fired recoilless rifle. Remember, the M20 Super Bazooka was also 3.54 inches in diameter, and it was a shoulder-fired weapon—not dissimilar to the weapon that followed it.

In addition, the Swedish-manufactured AT-4 antitank missile launcher used by the army and NATO forces resembles the bazooka in diameter (at 3.3 inches, or 84 mm) and shape. Where the M20 could penetrate 11 inches (28 cm) of tank armor, though, the AT-4 can reportedly penetrate about 15 inches (38 cm). The US Army was impressed by the Swedish weapon and ordered a slightly modified version, the M136, for their use.

A soldier demonstrates a recoilless shoulder-fired rifle in 1984. These types of guns, the successors of the M20 Super Bazooka, are still in use today.

The M72 LAW (light antitank weapon) is 2.6 inches (66 mm) in diameter and features a similar tube shape to the bazooka. Also like the M20, it can penetrate just over 11 inches (28 cm) of armor. The M72 was widely used in the Vietnam War and then suspended in the 1980s because of design issues that presented potential safety hazards. Also, the AT-4 was found to be more powerful, so it replaced the use of the M72 by the United States military—that is, until recently. The AT-4 isn't terribly suitable for urban combat, so the US Army and Marine Corps reinstated use of the M72 for combat in Iraq and Afghanistan. They did, however, order a revised and improved version of the weapon, which was completed in 2011.

The RPG-7 is a rocket-propelled grenade launcher used by Russia and other Warsaw Pact countries. It is, in fact, the most commonly used anti-armor weapon worldwide. Forty countries use the weapon, and it is particularly popular with guerrilla armies. Depending on the type of artillery used with it, the RPG-7 can penetrate up to about 20 inches (50 cm) of armor.

BODY ARMOR TODAY

Body armor comes in many forms and is always being revised and improved upon. In the Korean War era, there were two goals: create a more bulletproof body armor, and create a lighter-weight body armor. The flak vests designed during the Korean War generally weighed about 10 to 12 pounds (4.5 to 5.4 kg) and were somewhat bulletproof—but certainly not foolproof in that respect.

Technology took a bit of a step backward in the weight department, though. Currently, the US Army favors the Improved Outer Tactical Vest (IOTV), which is loaded with ballistic plates and weighs about 31 pounds (14 kg). It's heavy, but it is designed for flexibility and ease of use. It's easy to put on and easy to remove—at least, as easy as any 30-pound (13.6 kg) garment can be! It also features a hidden release lanyard, which allows the IOTV to release immediately into pieces for quick removal. The IOTV is also designed somewhat for **ergonomic** comfort. Whereas older vests forced the wearer to bear the weight on his or her shoulders, the IOTV distributes the weight to the lower torso. In terms of being bulletproof, the IOTV is quite strong. In addition to the ballistic plates, it uses Kevlar panels that can stop a 9 mm bullet traveling at up to 1,400 feet per second (426 meters per second).

However, the IOTV may not be used for much longer. Going back to its goal of a lighter-weight option, the US Army plans to test a new type of body armor known as Torso and Extremities Protection (TEP). If the tests are favorable, the army hopes to roll out the TEP system in 2019. Initial tests within the Army and Marines have indicated a 95 percent satisfaction rate. The TEP system will weigh about 23 pounds (10 kg), compared to the IOTV's 31 pounds (14 kg). It will be coupled with new body armor plates and a new helmet system.

Body Armor to Protect Officers and Civilians

Body armor isn't just for military use! It's now used for police officers, certain emergency services workers, and even civilian applications (such as protective gear for motorcycle riders). In these nonmilitary uses, the "armor" of choice is often Kevlar. Kevlar itself is a proper

Body armor is worn by peace officers and civilians when the situation calls for it.

name for a synthetic fiber manufactured by DuPont—just like Kleenex is the proper name for a particular brand of facial tissue. There are other similar fibers manufactured: Nomex is another one (also manufactured by DuPont), as is Technora (manufactured by the Japanese company Teijin), but just like the word Kleenex is sometimes used to describe any facial tissue, the word Kevlar is often casually used to describe fibers of that type. Kevlar is incredibly strong, so it is used in products that require significant strength, such as racing tires, drum heads, frying pans, and—you guessed it—body armor.

Kevlar is essentially like an incredibly strong gauze—it is a **polymer** that consists of millions of cross-linked chains. Because the cross-linking among chains is so intricate, the chains are nearly impossible to separate from one another, making it pretty much the strongest gauze-like material imaginable. Kevlar layers these cross-linked polymer chains for a material so strong that it can stop a bullet at great speed. Of course, there are weapons and ammunition capable of penetrating Kevlar, but not many—if you wear a Kevlar vest and you get shot, there's a fairly high likelihood that the bullet will not penetrate the vest.

Kevlar is also quite lightweight compared to traditional body armor. A Kevlar vest can weigh as little as 5 to 8 pounds (2.3 to 3.6 kg). However, the body armor is not particularly comfortable to wear, despite its light weight.

BLOOD STORAGE, LIFE FLIGHTS, AND MODERN-DAY MASH UNITS

The fields of medicine and health care are constantly evolving. People are living longer, healthier lives thanks to the advances in health care, and injuries that once were life threatening can often be survived now.

Blood Banks

Blood banks existed during World War II, but not in an organized fashion for military purposes. Blood banking and plasma storage

US soldiers place vats of donated blood onto a truck during World War II.

was a new concept during that war, and it was refined and formalized during the Korean War, when the armed forces and the American Red Cross worked together to establish a constant blood and plasma supply that could sustain the transfusion supply needs in the event of a disaster or war.

That trend has continued. After running into blood shortages during World War II, it was evident that a system needed to be established to ensure that such a shortage was never encountered again. Even in peacetime and times without a natural disaster, the American Red Cross reports that annually, nearly five million people get blood transfusions.

During the Korean War, blood was donated and stored as whole blood and as plasma. Now, blood banks collect and store blood in several categories: red blood cells, **platelets**, and plasma. This allows physicians to use the particular component of blood that will most effectively help their patients.

AABB, which was formerly called the American Association of Blood Banks, now accredits blood-donation centers, such as American Red Cross facilities, hospitals, and certain other blood-collection facilities. America's Blood Centers is an organization of nonprofit community blood centers. Between the two organizations, people wanting to donate blood can find a reputable facility in which to do so. In addition, the armed forces themselves have an Armed Services Blood Program to support collection among military personnel.

The American Red Cross and some other blood-collection facilities also offer bloodmobiles, which are mobile blood donation centers. They are primarily used at colleges, high schools, and places of employment to provide an easy, convenient place for people to donate blood.

Medical Air Transports

Air transport was used for emergency medical care as far back as the 1870s, but it wasn't widely used until the Korean War, when helicopters began to be used for medical transport from the battlefield to a hospital or treatment facility.

Air ambulance medical transports are widely used today—and not just in military situations. Major trauma hospitals generally have helicopter landing pads on the roof or adjacent to them to allow critically ill patients to be flown in. When a regular ambulance ride may put a critical patient's life in jeopardy, a helicopter can be used for quick transport—such as from an accident scene or in the case of a newborn baby with a critical health condition who needs to be cared for in a specialized **NICU**. Also, insurance companies may charter flights to transport patients who become ill or injured when traveling out of the country. These air ambulance flights go by different names—life flights, mercy flights, and nonemergency medical transportation flights.

During the Korean War, the transportation was crude, to say the least. Sometimes patients were secured in basket stretchers attached to the helicopter landing gears. Other times they could be placed inside the cabin, but due to space limitations the patient's lower legs often stuck out through the doors. The air ambulances served as a means to an end: Medical care didn't happen on board; the helicopter was simply a vessel to transport the patient from Point A to Point B.

Nowadays, medical aircraft are equipped with devices to monitor and treat the patients they're transporting. They typically have CPR equipment, EKG machines, ventilators, and some medications—and patients no longer have to ride with their legs sticking out the door!

The type of aircraft used for air ambulances varies. Often they are helicopters of different types, but airplanes are used for some transports, too. Small Lear jets and similar types can be used for transport, and larger jumbo jets are sometimes used for "heavy lift" transports. Helicopters have the advantage of maneuverability. An airplane, whether large or small, always needs a runway or landing strip for takeoff and landing. On the other hand, because helicopters take off and land vertically, they can land on basically any flat surface that is free from obstructions. When rescue crews are trying to reach a critical victim on a battlefield or at an accident scene, there often isn't time to reach the victim with a traditional ambulance and transport him or her to an airport. A helicopter ensures quick, easy access. Plus, the helicopter can land directly at the trauma hospital, negating the need for a traditional ambulance transport from the airport to the hospital in question.

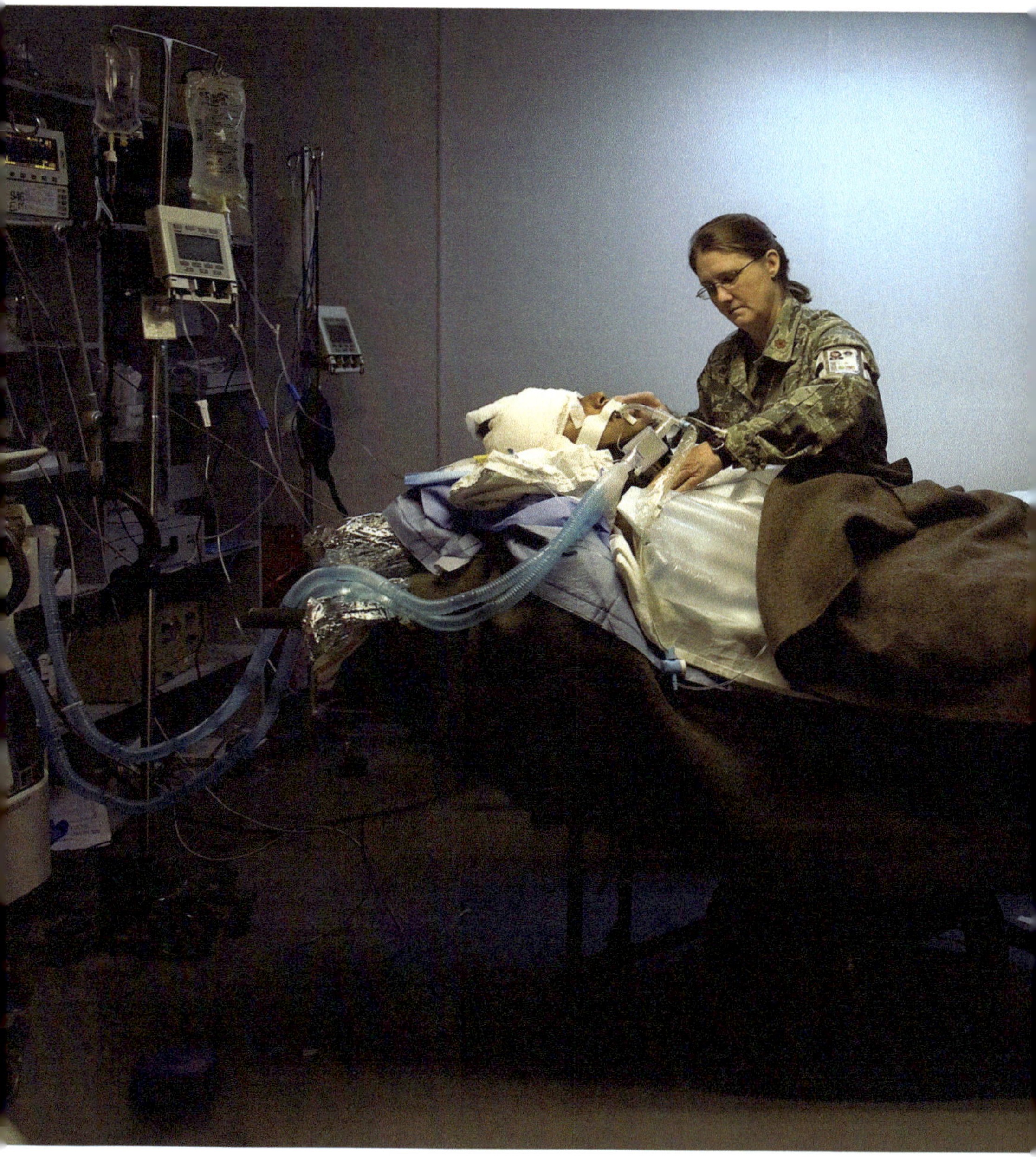

Today's MASH units are now called combat support hospitals, like this one in Afghanistan in 2008.

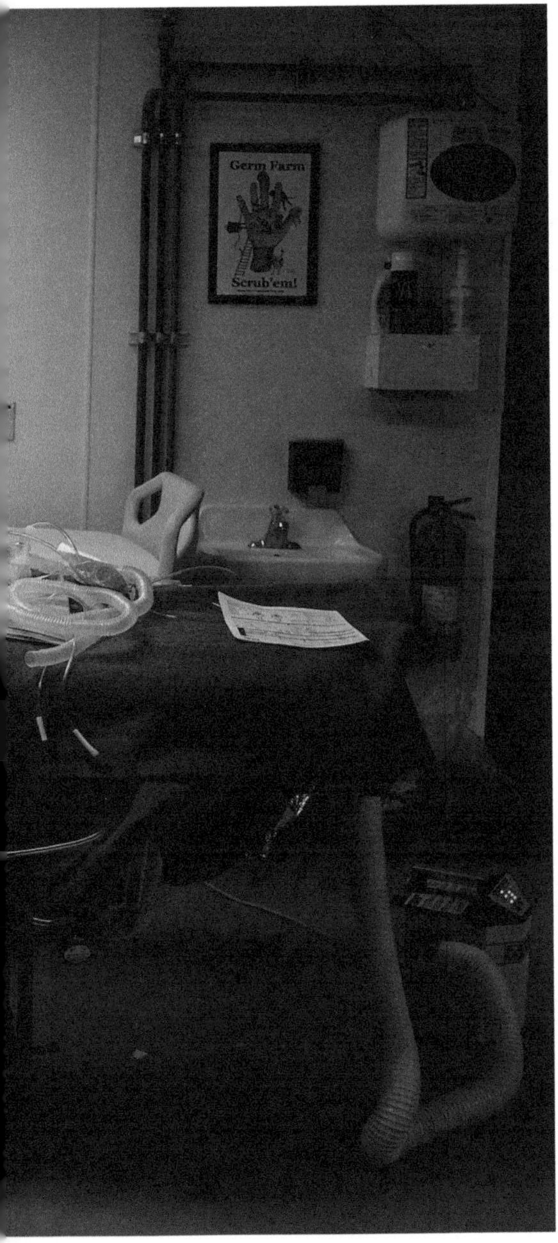

Combat Support Hospitals

MASH units were widely used during the Korean War, and they continued to be used up until 2006. In fact, the last MASH unit in South Korea was actually in operation until 1997, despite the war having ended nearly fifty years earlier! MASH units were used in Vietnam and later in the Gulf War.

Naturally, as medical facilities evolved and improved in their capabilities, so too did MASH units. The last MASH unit was deactivated in 2006, but MASH units continue to exist in part as combat support hospitals. Like MASH units, CSHs are mobile and can be set up in any combat or disaster zone and modified as needed. However, CSHs offer a bit more in terms of care than MASH units did. MASH units were primarily for trauma—

they were surgical centers to take care of critically ill or injured people—but CSHs are more like full-service hospitals. In addition to trauma care, they offer primary care, such as family practice doctors, obstetricians, and pediatricians.

While MASH units essentially stabilized critically wounded or ill patients for transport to other facilities, CSHs are more one-stop operations. They have the capacity to house patients for several days, so in theory a patient can be treated and released from the CSH rather than transported to a separate facility. This enables wounded soldiers to get back to their units more quickly, assuming their injuries aren't such that they need to be discharged from service.

LOOKING FORWARD

In the future, there's no doubt that the innovations of the Korean War will continue to be developed and refined. Air ambulances will continue to transport critically ill or injured patients, probably with enhanced health care support. Blood banks will continue to collect and store blood so it's available for transfusions when needed. Combat support hospitals will continue to offer medical treatment and services to military personnel—undoubtedly with the same updates and improvements in care that the rest of the medical community sees.

Bulletproof vests and body armor will continue to be refined, and as models become lighter and more usable, it's likely that they will continue to be used for civilian purposes outside of body protection against guns and knives. Also, unless war goes away for good—which we all know is unlikely—the rocket launcher technology developed for the bazooka will likely continue to inform weapons design for years to come.

That's the beauty of technology—it continues to evolve and unfold in ways that can enhance and improve our lives. Technology isn't always used for good—certainly, some uses of weapons are decidedly negative, for example—but it *can* be used for good when put in the right hands. Hopefully, that is a trend we will continue to see in future generations.

Bulletproof vest designs continue to be improved.

GLOSSARY

American Dream In the 1950s, the collective American Dream was for the head of the household (almost always a man) to have a good job, a perfect family, and a nice home, usually in the suburbs.

amphibious Taking place both on land and in water.

armistice Similar to a truce, an armistice is an agreement made to stop the fighting between opposing sides.

burp gun A submachine gun that could fire nine hundred rounds a minute and made an unusual sound while firing. The Soviet-designed PPSh-41 is an example of this type of gun.

counterculture A group whose attitudes about life are in opposition to the beliefs of the general public. During the 1960s, members of the counterculture were particularly vocal in their antiwar sentiments.

ergonomic Designed for comfort and efficiency.

fuselage An aircraft's main body piece.

HEAT rockets The acronym stands for high-explosive antitank rockets; they were used during the Korean War to try to damage tank armor.

hemolytic Involving the destruction or rupturing of red blood cells.

Iron Curtain An imagined barrier between the Communist Eastern Bloc and the non-Communist Western Bloc.

K rations Individual daily food rations given to soldiers during the war.

Leninism A political theory created by Soviet leader Vladimir Lenin, Leninism developed from Marxism and is a socialist political system that advocated for the working class to achieve political independence.

Marxism A political theory based on the ideas of Karl Marx and Friedrich Engels, Marxism is a Communist political system in which there are no class divisions and society governs itself.

mortar A short-range bomb fired from a short, smooth-bore gun at a high angle.

NATO The acronym stands for North Atlantic Treaty Organization. NATO is a group of countries that work together as a military alliance to mount a mutual defense in response to an attack by a non-NATO organization or country.

NICU The acronym stands for neonatal intensive care unit and refers to an area in a hospital where premature and newborn infants are cared for.

platelets A component of blood; platelets are involved in clotting.

polymer A series of bonded units that form interconnected chains.

rice paddy A field that is flooded in order for rice to be grown.

Warsaw Pact A defense treaty signed by the Soviet Union and seven other Communist states in Central and Eastern Europe.

BIBLIOGRAPHY

"Armored Vest Fact Sheet." US Army Quartermaster Museum. December 23, 1952. http://www.qmmuseum.lee.army.mil/korea/armored_vest.htm.

"The ASBP, Over 50 Years of Giving." Armed Services Blood Program. http://www.militaryblood.dod.mil/About/50_years.aspx.

"Bazooka Co-Inventor Edward Uhl Dies at 92." CBS News, May 13, 2010. http://www.cbsnews.com/news/bazooka-co-inventor-edward-uhl-dies-at-92.

"Blood Banking & Donation." American Society of Hematology. http://www.hematology.org/Patients/Basics/Banking.aspx.

"Body Armor (Flak Jackets) in WW II." Olive-Drab. http://olive-drab.com/od_soldiers_gear_body_armor_wwii.php.

"Body Armor History." Global Security. http://www.globalsecurity.org/military/systems/ground/body-armor2.htm.

"Bombing of Hiroshima and Nagasaki." History.com. http://www.history.com/topics/world-war-ii/bombing-of-hiroshima-and-nagasaki.

"A Brief History of the American Red Cross." American Red Cross. http://www.redcross.org/about-us/who-we-are/history.

"By the Numbers: World-Wide Deaths." The National WWII Museum. http://www.nationalww2museum.org/learn/education/for-students/ww2-history/ww2-by-the-numbers/world-wide-deaths.html.

"C-47 Skytrain." Global Security. http://www.globalsecurity.org/military/systems/aircraft/c-47.htm.

"Charles Richard Drew: Father of the Blood Bank." American Chemical Society. http://www.acs.org/content/acs/en/education/whatischemistry/african-americans-in-sciences/charles-richard-drew.html.

"The Cold War." John F. Kennedy Presidential Library and Museum. http://www.jfklibrary.org/JFK/JFK-in-History/The-Cold-War.aspx.

Cosgrove-Mather, Bootie. "TV Guide Names Top 50 Shows." CBS News, April 26, 2002. http://www.cbsnews.com/news/tv-guide-names-top-50-shows.

Dailey, Edward C. *MacArthur's X Corps in Korea: Ischon to the Yalu 1950*. Nashville, TN: Turner, 1999.

Dawson, Debi. "Army to Field Improved Body Armor." US Army, April 2, 2007. http://www.army.mil/article/2497/army-to-field-improved-body-armor.

Di Liddo, Deidre, and Emma George Hewett. "Body Armor." *Scientia Review*. http://www.scientiareview.org/pdfs/260.pdf.

Dunstan, Simon. *Flak Jackets: Twentieth-Century Military Body Armor.* Oxford, UK: Osprey, 1984.

Fitzgerald, Brian. *The Korean War: America's Forgotten War.* North Mankato, MN: Compass Point Books, 2006.

"Flak Jacket." Korean War Online. http://www.koreanwaronline.com/arms/flak.htm.

Former members of Task Force Smith. Letter to President Reagan on failure of 2.36-inch bazooka. 1985.

Frank, Lisa Tendrich, ed. *An Encyclopedia of American Women at War*. Santa Barbara, CA: ABC-CLIO, LLC, 2013.

"General Douglas MacArthur (1880–1964)." American Experience. http://www.pbs.org/wgbh/amex/macarthur/peopleevents/pandeAMEX96.html.

Greenhouse, Steven. "Edward Uhl, Who Helped Invent Bazooka, Dies at 92." *New York Times*, May 16, 2010. http://www.nytimes.com/2010/05/17/business/17uhl.html?_r=0.

"History of Air Ambulance and Medevac." Mercy Flight Western New York. http://www.mercyflight.org/content/pages/medevac.

"A History of the Army Blood Program." Armed Services Blood Program. http://www.militaryblood.dod.mil/About/army_history.aspx?tb=1.

Jahnera, Kyle. "Army to Roll Out Better Body Armor, Combat Shirt in 2019." *USA Today*, February 24, 2016. http://www.usatoday.com/story/news/nation-now/2016/02/24/army-combat-shirt-body-armor-2019/80851048.

James, D. Clayton. "Douglas MacArthur." Encyclopedia Britannica. http://www.britannica.com/biography/Douglas-MacArthur.

June, Christine. "Army's Last MASH Becomes a CSH." US Army, October 18, 2006. http://www.army.mil/article/385/Army__039_s_last_MASH_becomes_a_CSH.

Kendrick, Douglas B. "The Blood, Plasma, and Related Programs in the Korean War." From *Blood Program in World War II, Supplemented by Experiences in the Korean War*. US Army Office of Medical History. http://history.amedd.army.mil/booksdocs/wwii/blood/chapter20.htm.

"Kevlar Brand." DuPont. http://www.dupont.com/products-and-services/fabrics-fibers-nonwovens/fibers/brands/kevlar.html.

"Kevlar Inventor Stephanie Kwolek Dies." BBC News, June 21, 2014. http://www.bbc.com/news/world-us-canada-27951043.

King, Booker, and Ismail Jatoi. "The Mobile Army Surgical Hospital (MASH): A Military and Surgical Legacy." *Journal of the National Medical Association* 97, no. 5 (May 5, 2005): 648–656. http://www.ncbi.nlm.nih.gov/pmc/articles/PMC2569328/pdf/jnma00186-0014.pdf.

"Korean War." History.com. http://www.history.com/topics/korean-war.

Lewis, Jack. *The Gun Digest Book of Assault Weapons*. 6th edition. Fort Collins, CO: Krause Publications, 20014.

Malkasian, Carter. *The Korean War*. New York: Rosen, 2008.

"M.A.S.H. Medevac Helicopters." Century of Flight. http://www.century-of-flight.net/Aviation%20history/helicopter%20history/M.A.S.H.%20Medevac%20Helicopters.htm.

"M20 3.5in Rocket Launcher and Manuals." Korean War Online. http://www.koreanwaronline.com/arms/bazsup.htm.

"M20 3.5-Inch Rocket Launcher (Bazooka)." Global Security. http://www.globalsecurity.org/military/systems/ground/m20-bazooka.htm.

"101 Best Written TV Series." Writers Guild of America, West. http://wga.org/content/default.aspx?id=4925.

Pazzanese, Christina. "The Talented Georges Doriot." *Harvard Gazette*, February 24, 2015. http://news.harvard.edu/gazette/story/2015/02/the-talented-georges-doriot.

Rhem, Kathleen T. "Korean War Death Stats Highlight Modern DoD Safety Record." US Department of Defense, June 8, 2000. https://web.archive.org/web/20120114121831.

Rothman, Lily. "How the Korean War Started." *Time*, June 25, 2015. http://time.com/3915803/korean-war-1950-history.

"US Strategic Bombing Survey: The Effects of the Atomic Bombings of Hiroshima and Nagasaki, June 19, 1946." Harry S. Truman Library & Museum. http://www.trumanlibrary.org/whistlestop/study_collections/bomb/large/documents/index.php?pagenumber=14&documentid=65&documentdate=1946-06-19.

Zimmerman, Dwight Jon. "Battlefield Medicine in the Korean War." Defense Media Network, February 9, 2014. http://www.defensemedianetwork.com/stories/battlefield-medicine-in-the-korean-war.

FURTHER INFORMATION

Websites

The Korean War

http://www.history.army.mil/reference/korea/kw-chrono.htm

The US Army maintains this website with a chronology of events of the Korean War.

The Korean War and Its Origins

www.trumanlibrary.org/whistlestop/study_collections/koreanwar/index.php

The Truman Library offers a comprehensive list of links to documents related to the Korean War.

Korean War Project

www.koreanwar.org

The Korean War Project is a free website full of links related to the Korean War. There are databases, maps, reference links, and more.

Korean War Records

www.archives.gov/research/military/korean-war

The National Archives offers a military records page dedicated to the Korean War, with casualty lists, MIA (missing in action) lists, and searchable electronic records.

62 Interesting Facts About the Korean War

http://facts.randomhistory.com/korean-war-facts.html

If you're a fan of trivia, this site is full of interesting, random facts about the Korean War.

Videos

Crash Course US History: The Cold War and Asia

https://www.youtube.com/watch?v=Y2IcmLkuhGO&list=PL8dPuuaLjX
tMwmepBjTSG593eG7ObzO7s&index=39

This brief animated video, hosted by best-selling author John Green, describes the Korean War, the Vietnam War, and the United States during the 1950s, 1960s, and 1970s.

The History: Korean War

https://www.youtube.com/watch?v=R9J3k9a_G2s

This forty-minute documentary showcases the main events of the Korean War.

Korea: The Forgotten War

This four-DVD set tells the complete story of the Korean War.

Korean War Stories

Walter Cronkite and Buzz Aldrin are among the famous names who lend their talents to this DVD telling the stories of the men involved in the Forgotten War.

Korean War Videos

www.history.com/topics/korean-war/videos

History.com offers several short streaming videos about the Korean War.

INDEX

Page numbers in **boldface** are illustrations. Entries in **boldface** are glossary terms.

ABOUT THE AUTHOR

Cathleen Small is an author and editor. She has written numerous books for students in grades 3 through 12. Her interest in technology goes back decades, to when she grew up in the Silicon Valley in the midst of the Apple/IBM tech war, and continued as she worked as an editor for technical publications for more than a decade. When she's not writing or editing, Small enjoys spending time with her two young sons and her husband, as well as traveling to places far and near.